T0318500

Cambridge Elements ≣

Elements in Pragmatics
edited by
Jonathan Culpeper
Lancaster University
Michael Haugh
University of Queensland, Australia

POSITIVE SOCIAL ACTS

A Metapragmatic Exploration of the Brighter and Darker Sides of Sociability

Roni Danziger
Hebrew University of Jerusalem

Shaftesbury Road, Cambridge CB2 8EA, United Kingdom

One Liberty Plaza, 20th Floor, New York, NY 10006, USA

477 Williamstown Road, Port Melbourne, VIC 3207, Australia

314–321, 3rd Floor, Plot 3, Splendor Forum, Jasola District Centre,
New Delhi – 110025, India

103 Penang Road, #05–06/07, Visioncrest Commercial, Singapore 238467

Cambridge University Press is part of Cambridge University Press & Assessment,
a department of the University of Cambridge.

We share the University's mission to contribute to society through the pursuit of
education, learning and research at the highest international levels of excellence.

www.cambridge.org
Information on this title: www.cambridge.org/9781009184427

DOI: 10.1017/9781009184410

First published 2022

A catalogue record for this publication is available from the British Library.

ISBN 978-1-009-18442-7 Paperback
ISSN 2633-6464 (online)
ISSN 2633-6456 (print)

Positive Social Acts

A Metapragmatic Exploration of the Brighter and Darker Sides of Sociability

Elements in Pragmatics

DOI: 10.1017/9781009184410
First published online: December 2022

Roni Danziger
Hebrew University of Jerusalem
Author for correspondence: Roni Danziger, roni.danziger@mail.huji.ac.il

Abstract: Sociability is friendly behavior that is performed by a variety of positive social acts that are aimed to establish, promote, or restore relationships. However, attempts to achieve these interactional goals can fail or backfire; moreover, interactants may abuse these strategies. A pragmatic focus on positive social acts illuminates the ways they succeed in promoting sociability and why they sometimes fail to enhance social relations. This Element analyzes positive social actions receiving positive and negative metapragmatic labels, such as *firgun* and flattery, in the Hebrew-speaking community in Israel. Adopting a metapragmatic methodology enables a differentiation between positive communication and its evaluation as (in)appropriate in context. The Conclusion discusses the fuzzy line between acceptable and unacceptable positive behavior and the benefits and perils of deploying positive social acts in interaction. It also suggests a conceptualization of the darker and brighter sides of sociability as intrinsically connected, rather than polar ends.

Keywords: positive communication, sociability, metapragmatics, over-politeness, Hebrew

ISBNs: 9781009184427 (PB), 9781009184410 (OC)
ISSNs: 2633-6464 (online), 2633-6456 (print)

Contents

1 Introduction

In his treatise on ethics, Aristotle claims that moral life is comprised of virtues and vices, each of which represent an expression of action or feeling on a continuum of excess ↔ mean ↔ deficiency. Virtues are mean expressions, while vices are extreme expressions. For example, confidence is best articulated as courage, but, in excess, it is expressed through rashness; deficiency of action is cowardice. In the same vein, in the sphere of social conduct, friendliness is a virtue, while the result of deficiency is the vice of cantankerousness (or in plainer language, being an antisocial grump), and the result of excess is obsequiousness (ingratiation). There are many metapragmatic terms for being too friendly, such as sycophantic, creepy, groveling, servile, schmoozing, unctuous, and idealizing. These are the more standardized versions of the blunter, everyday terms such as ass-kissing, apple-polishing, brown-nosing, and sucking up. This semantic field of obsequiousness indicates that there is certainly such a thing as being too nice. But what does it mean to be nice or too nice? What social actions are considered friendly behavior and when are they considered excessive, unacceptable, or inappropriate? And where is the line crossed? This Element aims to answer these questions by exploring the "brighter" and "darker" sides of sociability.

In the social sciences, sociability is generally used to describe conscious and unconscious initiating of social relations and interpersonal bonds in a given context (Ninomiya, 2001). I use "bright" and "dark" to describe acceptable and unacceptable use of positive communication to advance sociability, respectively. I will not cover unacceptable *negative* behavior (e.g., impoliteness, rudeness, insults, threats, etc.). Additionally, although various forms of negative behaviors such as argument, impoliteness, and mockery can, in certain contexts, be solidarity enhancing or sociability promoting (e.g., Schiffrin, 1984; Haugh, 2010; Culpeper, 2011), the focus of this Element is *positive* social acts.

Originating from the Latin *positivuus* (past participle of *ponere* – "to put" or "to place"), meaning "settled by agreement," the adjective "positive" came to English from the Old French *positif*, a legal term meaning "formally laid down, or imposed, prescribed." The adjective has evolved greatly from the early fourteenth century and has several meanings in modern English, such as "hopeful," "certain," "useful," "expressing agreement or support," and "confident and successful." In light of the common ground these meanings share and the everyday use of "positive," I will use it to mean "conventionally seen as good" in various ways.[1]

---

[1] See the definitions given in *Cambridge Dictionary*, Cambridge Dictionaries Online website (https://dictionary.cambridge.org/us/dictionary/english/positive); *Oxford Advanced Learner's*

This Element is organized as follows: It will first define and exemplify positive social acts, positive communication, and polite communication by reviewing and discussing the relevant literature in the field of pragmatics. Section 2 will clarify the choice of a metapragmatic methodology for the collection and analysis of positive social acts. Sections 3 and 4, respectively, describe and explain the bright side of sociability, that is, positive social acts that are evaluated as appropriate, polite, and acceptable, and its dark side, that is, positive social actions that are evaluated as inappropriate, over-polite, or unacceptable. The data used has been collected mainly from the Hebrew-speaking community in Israel. Studies have been conducted on positive communication in the Hebrew-speaking community in Israel (e.g., Katriel, 1993; Danziger, 2018; Kampf & Danziger, 2019) that will enable an analysis of acceptable and unacceptable use of positive communication in this context.

1.1 The Sections in This Element

In Section 2, I will argue that friendly behavior is performed through a variety of positive social acts that can be organized under a "pragmatic field" of social behaviors designed to establish, promote, or restore relationships. I will outline that which can be referred to as positive communication and suggest that it is related to, but differs from, polite communication, even though, in pragmatics, the two are sometimes conflated. The first is action-based, while the latter is evaluation-based.

Section 3 will focus on the bright side of sociability, that is, positive social actions that are evaluated as appropriate, polite, and acceptable and therefore can potentially achieve sociability. This section will offer a corpus-based analysis of positive actions, metapragmatically labeled as *firgun*, that is, culturally approved positive communication in the Hebrew-speaking community in Israel. The metapragmatic label of *firgun* is an umbrella term that describes sincere and supportive relational work, which has become the prism through which positive communication is understood and enacted by Hebrew speakers (Katriel, 1993; Danziger, 2018; Danziger & Kampf, 2021). Findings will demonstrate how text, context, and the moral order are drawn upon to form culture-specific interpretations of positive communication.

Section 4 will focus on the dark side of sociability, that is, positive social actions that are evaluated as inappropriate, over-polite, or unacceptable. Consequently, these actions may fail to achieve sociability. This exploratory section will analyze metapragmatically labeled behaviors of overly positive

---

Dictionary, Oxford Learner's Dictionaries website (www.oxfordlearnersdictionaries.com/definition/english/positive_1?q=positive); and *Merriam-Webster Dictionary* website (www.merriam-webster.com/dictionary/positive#h1) (accessed February 21, 2022).

communication. First, it will establish the semantic-pragmatic field of positive communication commonly perceived as negative in English, such as schmoozing, ingratiating, obsequiousness, servility, and so on. Second, it will describe contexts in which positive social acts are negatively evaluated and provide illustrative examples for each, either collected for this Element or drawn from other studies of over-politeness. Lastly, it will analyze two examples in Hebrew and Arabic, where positive social acts were evaluated negatively, due to the disadvantageous context of the intractable Israeli-Palestinian conflict.

The Conclusion will discuss the fuzzy line between acceptable and unacceptable positive behavior and the benefits and perils of deploying positive acts in social interactions. It will embrace the fuzziness of social relations, which are dynamic and relative by nature, and visualize sociability as a Möbius strip with two seemingly separate poles that, in reality, function as the inverse and obverse of the same structural surface. The only way to grasp their relation is by constantly shifting our perspective between the two points. Conceptualizing sociability as a Möbius strip implies that perhaps it is not enough to try to distinguish between its brighter and darker sides. To grasp the complexity of sociability, it may be helpful to see these two sides as inseparable, intertwined, and perhaps defining one another.

The purpose of this Element is to explore the category of positive social acts, define them, and describe their use, function, and interpretation. While positive social acts were studied in various contexts in previous pragmatic studies, as an analytic category in their own right they are under-researched. Highlighting positive social acts as a category in the vast field of social interaction – or in Goodwin's (1994) "professional vision" terms, drawing the line around positive social acts in the infinite sand of social interaction – gives them the status of an object of knowledge worthy of academic study. What makes them worthy of academic study is how they illuminate the fundamentals of sociability and the role of language in advancing, or derailing, it. The sections in this Element are devised in a fashion that will adequately promote an understanding of what positive social acts are and when they achieve or fail to achieve their ends, of advancing sociability. This analytic plan does not fit the traditional length of a journal submission, but it also will not fill the pages of a typical book. Therefore, the topic is offered to the readers as an Element in pragmatics. In this manner, the category of positive social acts receives its proper framing within the study of social interaction.

2 What Are Positive Social Acts?

Positive social acts can be categorized as describing language, actions, and behaviors that are conventionally regarded as positive in interaction, that is, as promoting sociability. Among these are actions that are considered face-enhancing, friendly, or as promoting relationships. In academic life, for example, we often present our work in class or in international conferences. If someone were to come up to us and tell us that our presentation was very interesting, that would likely make us happy. Perhaps we would reciprocate by thanking that kind person. This type of interaction may lead to the inception of a work relationship, or even a personal one.

What exactly falls under the category of positive social acts? Expressive speech acts are obvious candidates: compliments, praise, congratulations, good wishes, thanks, and redressive actions (e.g., apologies). Each of these speech acts have been thoroughly studied in pragmatics and have been found to promote sociability in various ways. Compliments are said to promote solidarity (e.g., Holmes, 1986); redressive actions restore affected relationships (e.g., Kampf, 2008); and thanks realign them (Ohashi, 2008). Of course, not all expressives are positive social actions. Expressives like reproach, deplore, protest, and accuse are speech acts that convey the negative feelings or psychological state of the speaker (Wierzbicka, 1987; Vandervaken, 1990). Conversely, illocutions that reflect a positive psychological state presumably lead to a more sociable state of affairs.

Positive social acts can also be speech acts from other illocutionary categories (Searle, 1976) if they can potentially create a positive effect. Thus, for example, commissive speech acts such as a promise to behave better in the future or an offer to help someone move in, a directive speech act such as a request for cooperation, or a representative speech act such as the assertion of friendship can all promote sociability. Kampf, Heimann, and Aldar (2022) explain how the representative speech act of assertion of friendship has a bidirectional fit of world-to-word (Searle, 1976). Thus, by publicly asserting that "America has no greater friend then Israel," the former Israeli prime minister Benjamin Netanyahu not only describes a state of affairs he believes to be true but also constitutes this friendship by signaling his desire for a friendly relationship with his US counterpart (Kampf et al., 2022: 653). In this very real-world example, we can see how positive speech acts can promote friendly relations.

Positive social acts are not exclusively "positive politeness" in the Brown and Levinson (1987) sense (to make the other feel appreciated and loved); they can promote either solidarity or deference ("negative politeness"), or both. An expression of deference can also be positive if it makes the other feel good (perhaps powerful or respected). This is not to say that their consequences are always the same but that the various illocutions and perlocutions of positive speech acts have the potential of making the other feel good. Thus, both the illocution of apology and the perlocution of forgiveness, as well as an illocution of congratulation and the perlocution of solidarity, have the potential to create a positive effect for the receiver. Kerbrat-Orecchioni (1997) terms these other-oriented actions "face enhancing acts," in contrast to Brown and Levinson's "face threatening acts." Kampf et al. (2019), who studied sociability in interstate relations using a combination of Brown and Levinson's (1987) framework and peace studies (Mitchell, 2000), call these speech acts "amicable actions" because they promote, establish, or restore interstate relationships.

The association between politeness and a focus on the other can be traced back to Leech (1983: 133), who saw it as "a general law" of politeness to formulate speech act performance by minimizing negative acts and maximizing positive acts. In this seminal work that has left a lasting mark on the field of pragmatics, the conflation of positive communication and polite communication is apparent. Like Kerbrat-Orecchioni (1997) and Brown and Levinson (1987), Leech's "Principles of Politeness" are also designed with regard to speech act performance. For example, he ascribed the Tact Maxim to impositives and commisives and the Modesty Maxim to expressives and assertives. Consequently, in pragmatics, speech acts are often placed at the center of social interaction.

Sociability, however, is not solely built on speech acts; various verbal and nonverbal social acts have been linked to positive communication. Conventional positive strategies such as seeking common ground, making someone laugh, using pet names and nicknames, expressing love and caring, and even gossiping can promote sociability (Brown & Levinson, 1987). Nonverbal behaviors can also play a role in advancing sociability – for example, paralinguistic markers, such as tone of voice; smiling and body language; and social actions, such as gift-giving, gestures, and favors. A recent study has shown that laughter in the context of intercultural conflictual workplace interactions can mitigate relational tension and facilitate reconciliation (Du, 2022).

2.1 Positive Communication

Positive social acts are the building blocks of positive communication. If communication has two main functions – transactional (information transferring) and interactional (maintenance of social relationships) (Brown & Yule, 1983) – then positive communication has the potential to establish, promote, and maintain social relations. Positive social acts are coded as conventionally good (speaker-oriented), but in order to achieve sociability, they need to be seen as such (hearer-oriented).

At this point, I would like to suggest that positive communication strategies are social behaviors that are aimed at making the other feel good. Goffman stipulates that "feeling good" happens if one has established a better face than expected in the interaction (Goffman, 1967: 6). While this assertion suggests that positively marked social behavior is an indication of successful impression management, leaving a good impression in interaction is not the only reason a person would "feel good." Feeling good can also derive from feeling appreciated, loved, thought of, respected, and so on. Of course, what makes us feel good varies according to personal as well as cultural values. For example, Barnlund and Araki (1985) have found that while a Japanese speaker often compliments a person's taste, American English speakers rarely give praise in this area. As it may be rare, a compliment on someone's taste (in fashion, for example) may be unexpected and therefore positively marked in American English (by this logic, it can also be negatively marked). In the Hebrew-speaking community in Israel, being an honest, straightforward person is highly valued, so compliments pertaining to sincerity are common in Israeli political discourse (Kampf & Danziger, 2019). Cultures that do not regard sincerity as a core value of their moral order may not find compliments of this kind so positive.[2]

Various works in the field of pragmatics have offered conceptualizations of sociability strategies. In their research on workplace relations, Holmes and Marra (2004) use the term "relational practice" (RP) to describe the two fundamental goals of relating in the workplace: first, establishing and maintaining solidarity and good relations; and second, "damage control" in the form of constructing and maintaining dignity, mitigating potentially threatening behaviors, and minimizing conflict. Spencer-Oatey (2000: 3) prefers to use the term "rapport management" to describe the management of interpersonal relations or the "use of language to promote, maintain or threaten harmonious social relations." In this framework, positive communication would fall under rapport enhancement and rapport maintenance orientations. Spencer-Oatey's rapport neglect and rapport challenge orientations are the opposite: They cause harm to harmonious relations, either by a lack of concern for sociability or by an active desire to impair it. These dichotomous attitudes are similarly described in conversation analysis (CA), where a "maximal pro-social" interaction oriented toward cooperation is referred to as "affiliation," while "disaffiliation" is a noncooperative orientation in conversation (for elaboration, see Steensig, 2020).

These categories of "brighter" and "darker" interactional orientations may invite associations between positive communication and politeness and negative communication and impoliteness. This Element will demonstrate that this common association is unproductive for studying sociability; moreover, it will propose an explicit separation between the two paradigms of positive social acts

---

[2] It is important to reiterate that despite the fact that cultures share a communication ethos, there will always be personal and subgroup variations, that is, not all members of a linguaculture will have the same perception of certain behaviors.

and their evaluation in context. This is a good point to start teasing out the difference between positive and polite communication. Positive communication includes other-oriented positive social actions, which are aimed at making the other feel good, enhancing face, or promoting sociability. Polite communication, however, is an evaluation of appropriateness of language and behavior in context (Spencer-Oatey, 2000; Locher & Watts, 2005). The next section will delve into polite communication and how it relates to, yet differs from, positive communication.

2.2 Polite Communication

Scholars of discursive approaches to politeness will often use different definitions for (im)politeness, but what they all have in common is the notion of relating (Locher & Watts, 2005; Arundale, 2006; Kádár & Haugh, 2013; Spencer-Oatey & Kádár, 2021). This underlying notion of relating highlights the interactional element of interpersonal relations (Locher & Graham, 2010) and explains why positive communication and polite communication are sometimes used interchangeably; they are both relational notions that are fundamental to interpersonal relationships. However, the first is action-based, whereas the latter is evaluation-based. For example, an expressive speech act is considered a compliment when it gives credit to the other for some "good" seen as such by both parties (Holmes, 1986). Whether that language coded as a compliment is considered appropriate or inappropriate to the context (polite or impolite) is a matter of interpretation and evaluation of textual cues and contextual clues (Weizman & Dascal, 1991; Spencer-Oatey & Kádár, 2021).[3] This point of distinction between positive communication and politeness helps to elucidate cases of over-politeness – in other words, language coded as positive communication that receives a metapragmatic label of inappropriateness (Locher & Watts, 2005).

The understanding that politeness is evaluative in nature began with Eelen's (2001) famous critique of conventional politeness theory. Inspired by his work, Spencer-Oatey and Kádár (2021: 3) claim that

> evaluation is fundamental to how politeness comes into existence, and in the body of politeness research it has even been argued that it is more important how we interpret politeness then how we produce it.

This means that any utterance can be considered polite or impolite, whether coded as positive or negative. The interpretation process of interactants takes

---

[3] Weizman and Dascal (1991: 21) suggest that when "readers" detect an "interpretation problem," that is, a meaning gap or mismatch, they look for textual cues (such as linguistic choices, missing elements, and possible implicatures) and contextual clues (contextual information about participants and general knowledge about interaction, truth conditions, social factors, etc.).

both text and context into consideration, but equally important, it also considers the specific social and cultural norms regarding appropriate and inappropriate language use in that linguaculture.

Recent works have drawn attention to an evaluation process in which judgment of language as polite or impolite draws on the culture and moral order of the participants in an interaction (e.g., Culpeper, 2011; Haugh, 2013; Kádár & Haugh, 2013; Danziger & Kampf, 2021; Spencer-Oatey & Kádár, 2021). Examples are numerous; variations in politeness norms across cultures have generated countless papers and books. However, one example has always stood out for me, because it demonstrates that cultural beliefs are sometimes hard to counteract even if the actors are aware of the differences between them: I am referring to the threat of the evil eye in relation to compliments and praise. In many South Asian, Middle Eastern, and Mediterranean cultures, people sometimes experience compliments and praise as negative because they invoke the evil eye and may result in harm to the object of the compliment. In Syrian Arabic, for example (but also in Jordanian, Palestinian, and Lebanese variations of Arabic), it is an act of solidarity to accompany these positive social actions with an expression meant to thwart the effect (yikhzi l-'een) (Nelson, El Bakary, & Al Batal, 1993). This social norm is not a mere curiosity; in diplomatic contexts, it can hinder successful interaction if some of the actors are unaware of the emotional implications these actions have in some cultures (Menon, Sheldon, & Galinsky, 2014).

Such variation in the underpinning of politeness (culture, text, and context) is further indication that not all positive social acts will necessarily be considered polite. By the same logic, negative communication such as mockery may be considered to be solidarity-promoting when it is performed in a jocular key (see Haugh, 2010). Second-wave discursive approaches to politeness and their application across cultures have demonstrated repeatedly that (im)politeness is a relative concept (e.g., Locher & Graham, 2010; Izadi, 2016; Spencer-Oatey & Kádár, 2021). The theory of relational work captures the relativity of impoliteness very well (e.g., Watts, 2003; Locher & Watts, 2005, 2008) because it explains politeness as "a discursive concept arising out of interactants' perceptions and judgments of their own and others' verbal behavior" (Locher & Watts, 2005: 10). Therefore, it will serve as the theoretical background for this Element.

2.3 Understanding Positive Social Actions through Relational Work Theory

Relational work is defined as "'work' individuals invest in negotiating relationships with others" (Locher & Watts, 2005: 10). Locher and Watts reject the implication in Brown and Levinson's (1987) politeness theory that some utterances are "polite" while others are "impolite," claiming that politeness and impoliteness are discursive concepts that are negotiated by speakers in a specific context and cannot be predetermined. In addition, Brown and Levinson assume that speakers always strive to maintain harmony, while Locher and Watts (2005) claim that speakers react to situations according to their social and linguistic knowledge, while their aim is not always to maintain harmony. For the latter, relational work includes all linguistic behavior: directness, politeness, impoliteness, rudeness, or aggression, which are all appropriate or inappropriate social behaviors. In their view, distinctions between politic and non-politic, or marked and unmarked behaviors, are more effective than solely politeness and impoliteness in understanding discourse and social interaction.

The theory describes a continuum of social interaction, most of which is unmarked, in other words, politic, or appropriate, to the context. Marked behavior is unexpected in context and commented on by participants in an interaction. This behavior can be negatively or positively marked; violations of expectations are commonly seen as negatively marked or impolite, such as the inappropriate use of language or a transgression of social norms. Positively marked behavior is likewise unexpected in context but in a good way, for instance, an especially moving birthday wish. According to this framework, appropriate/politic behavior is either expected in context (non-polite) or a positively marked interaction (polite).

The relational work continuum is circular, that is, over-polite behavior can cross into impoliteness. Over-politeness is a rather neglected part of the relational work continuum (see the following exceptions: Culpeper, 2008, 2011; Izadi, 2016; Danziger, 2020; Danziger & Kampf, 2021). It includes negatively marked behaviors, yet it is "not a case of rudeness," but rather "a less than optimal application of politeness patterns which in principle are perfectly acceptable in a given language or culture" (Kienpointner, 1997: 257). Negatively marked over-politeness could occur, for example, between individuals in an intimate relationship, where politeness strategies can be seen as unexpected and therefore hold impolite implicatures (Culpeper, 2011). The difference between an over-polite utterance and an impolite utterance lies in both (speaker-oriented) linguistic coding and (hearer-oriented) interpretation; over-politeness would be coded as positive and interpreted as negatively exceeding contextual expectations, while impoliteness would be coded as negative and interpreted as "seeking damage" (Culpeper, 2011: 1).

The relational work framework thus further aids in understanding the difference between positive and polite communication. Positive communication includes other-oriented positive social actions that seek to make the other feel good, enhance face, or promote sociability. Polite communication, however, is an evaluation of appropriateness of language and behavior in context (e.g., Spencer-Oatey, 2000; Locher & Watts, 2005). Through this distinction, positive social acts can be understood as the relational work individuals put into the "construction, maintenance, reproduction and transformation of interpersonal relationships among those engaged in social practice" (Locher & Watts, 2008: 96). The connection between positive and polite communication is at the center of interpersonal pragmatics, a subfield of pragmatics that deals with the relational side of language and its use. Interpersonal pragmatics focuses on the "relational aspect of interactions between people that both affect and are affected by their understandings of culture, society, and their own and others' interpretations" (Locher & Graham, 2010: 2).

Metapragmatics is one way to gauge the interpersonal side of language and how this relates to its use in a community of practice. Studies in this field have shown how metalinguistic resources often connect linguistic behavior with the moral order (Cameron, 2004). A metapragmatic methodology allows for an empirical study based on evaluative labels used by members of a community in order to discover how they interpret and negotiate what is considered polite and what can be perceived as over-polite.2.3

2.4 Metapragmatics As a Methodological Pillar for This Element

Metapragmatics is the study of reflexive awareness of language use. The important role of meta-discourse in meaning-making processes and the constitution of interpretive communities has been explained and demonstrated by scholars of pragmatics (e.g., Caffi, 1998; Verschueren, 2000; Culpeper, 2011). Metapragmatics is crucial to understanding verbal behavior and forms of social actions because actors' interpretations become "part and parcel of what need[s] to be described and explained" (Verschueren, 2000: 445). The ability to identify what others are doing with language is the basis of human interaction (Tomasello, 1999). The process of meaning-making and identification of social actions is evident through metapragmatic comments and labels. Metapragmatic comments like "That is so nice of you!" are opinions about the pragmatic and social implications of utterances, their function, or indexical relations (Culpeper, 2011). Metapragmatic labels are behaviors that have a conventional code in a community of practice, such as schmoozing, groveling, and toadying. These labels encapsulate an evaluation of certain behaviors in context. If politeness is evaluative, then metapragmatic labels are essential for analyzing the perception of positive social acts as (in)appropriate – for example, labeling a certain compliment as flattery or an apology as appeasement. While there are quite a few works on the labeling of negative communication as impolite (e.g., Culpeper, 2011; Stapleton, 2020), not many studies have addressed positive (positively marked) or negative labeling (over-politeness; see exceptions Izadi, 2016; Danziger, 2020) of positive communication.

Given the fundamental role of metapragmatics in the performance and evaluation of sociability, the methodology of this Element is largely a meta-pragmatic one. Section 3 in this Element is a corpus study that will explore a metapragmatically labeled positive behavior in the Hebrew-speaking community in Israel, that of *firgun*. It is an umbrella term that describes a sincere and supportive relational work that has become the prism through which positive communication is understood and enacted in this linguaculture. Section 4 is an exploratory endeavor that will draw on English, Hebrew, Persian, and Arabic examples. First, it will propose a semantic field of metapragmatic labels for overly positive social actions in English by analyzing dictionary definitions of possible members of the category such as schmoozing, ingratiating, and toadying. Second, it will describe the contexts in which we are likely to find them and provide illustrative examples either drawn from previous works on over-politeness or obtained ad hoc for the purpose of this Element. Third, it will provide an example where positive social acts are negatively evaluated due to a specific disadvantageous context, the intractable Israeli-Palestinian conflict, where positive social act can even be more detrimental then aiding to a political relationship.

2.5 Summary

This section established the "semantic-pragmatic" field of positive social acts by surveying the previous literature on sociability, with the goal of pinpointing the difference between positive communication and polite communication. I have shown that positive communication includes other-oriented positive social actions designed to make the other feel good, enhance face, or promote sociability. Polite communication, however, is an evaluation of appropriateness of language and behavior in context. In order for positive communication to achieve its goal of advancing sociability, it must be perceived as positive. This is the point of contact between positive and polite communication: positive social acts are relational work that is evaluated in context. Understanding the similarities and differences between positive and polite communication sets the ground for discussing positive social acts that are positively marked as opposed to negatively marked ones. Equipped with clear definitions, we can now discuss the interpretation process that leads to each evaluation.

3 Positively Evaluated Positive Social Acts

This section offers an analysis of positive actions, metapragmatically labeled as *firgun*, that is, culturally approved positive communication in the Hebrew-speaking community in Israel. The label of *firgun* is a culture-specific keyword (Katriel, 1986, 1993) that describes sincere and supportive relational work. As an illustration, the following example is from mit4mit.co.il,[4] an Israeli website that lists wedding vendors such as DJs, hair stylists, venues, and so on, alongside real reviews from brides and grooms who have used their services. The following review, about a wedding venue that offers an all-inclusive package of wedding services (bar, catering, music, photographer, etc.) was written by a groom. He gave the venue a score of 100/100 and a rave review. He ended his recommendation with the following words:[5]

חשוב להגיד שוב שזה נשמע מאוד מוגזם מה שכתבתי אבל לא היתי כותב ולא היתי מבזבז אפילו שניה מזמני בשביל לפרגן למישהו שלא מגיע לו עד מאוד! ולכל מי שלקח חלק בקרנבל חתונה שהיתה שם מגיע את כל הפירגון שבעולם ויותר מזה מגיע לאנשים טובים אחרים להנות ממה שיש להם להציע כי הם לא רואים ממטר אף מקום אחר!

Ḥashuv lehagid shuv shezeh nishm'a me'od mugzam mah shekatavti 'aval lo' hayiti kotev velo' haiti mebazbez 'afilu shniyah mizmani bishvil lefargen lemishehu shelo' magi'a lo 'ad me'od! Velekol mi shelakaḥ ḥelek bakarnaval ḥatunah shehayita sham magia' 'et kol hafirgun sheba'olam veyoter mizeh magi'a la'anashim tovim 'aḥerim lehanot mimah sheyesh lahem lehatsi'a ki hem lo' ro'im mimeter 'af makom aḥer!

It is important to say again that what I wrote sounds very exaggerated, but I would not write, nor would I waste even a second of my time to [perform] *firgun* for someone who does not deserve it so much! And everyone who took part in that wedding carnival deserves all the *firgun* in the world and more than that, other good people deserve to enjoy what they have to offer because they are so much better than all the other venues!

In this recommendation post, the groom shows gratitude for the services he has received by publicly writing about his experience, and he praises and compliments the people who were responsible for the success of his wedding. He makes an effort to emphasize his sincerity by stating that his review is not an exaggeration: They are deserving of his *firgun*, and he would not waste his time posting anything less than such a rave review. The idea of reciprocity recurs throughout the post: The groom wants to show his gratitude by publicly praising the venue, which will increase their popularity, but he also does that as a service to other future brides and grooms. The labeling of his positive social action as *firgun* triggers the metapragmatic knowledge of the Hebrew readers, who know

---

[4] See the mit4mit.co.il website: www.mit4mit.co.il/reviews/5429a8d4ba07a9204ae8080d (accessed March 1, 2022).

[5] All examples in Hebrew were translated and transliterated by the author. Transliteration follows the Library of Congress Romanization tables available at www.loc.gov/catdir/cpso/roman.html (accessed February 16, 2022).

the functions of the keyword and its role in the community. This example also shows how *firgun* encapsulates a variety of positive social actions (gratitude, praise, complimenting, recommending) and its cultural importance to positive communication in Hebrew. Using a cultural keyword that functions as a metacommunicative term is a productive way to collect and analyze positive social acts. Because the term encapsulates both pragmatic and cultural knowledge, its emic analysis also demonstrates the culture-specific understanding of positive communication in a community. However, the positive social actions that are included in the umbrella term *firgun* are not culture-specific; this methodology is applicable in any other culture that has an emic term for positive communication.

The data for this section was collected through SketchEngine.com, which offers a web-based dataset. Sketch Engine's algorithm harvests texts from web sources, such as blogs, news, and personal websites, and processes them into ready-to-use corpora, offering several analysis tools like concordances, frequency lists, and collocations. The corpus used for this section is HenTenTen14; it contains 890,282,843 Hebrew words collected from the web. Using a metacommunicative corpus search method (Jucker & Taavitsainen, 2014), items were collected and analyzed in order to gauge what positive social actions have received the label of *firgun*. Analyzing positive social acts that have been given the label of *firgun* serves the purpose of this section because it ensures a discussion of positively marked social behavior, that is, a positively coded social action and a positive evaluation of its performance in context. The following analysis and findings demonstrate the gamut of positive social actions and the way in which text, context, and sociocultural norms are drawn upon to form an evaluation of appropriate use of language that is positively marked. By analyzing instances of positive social acts being evaluated positively, we can better understand the "brighter" side of sociability, or how positive social acts can advance social relations.

3.1 Positive Communication in the Hebrew-Speaking Community in Israel

Pragmatic literature on positive social actions in modern Hebrew includes the examination of expressive speech acts like apologies (Blum-Kulka & Olshtain, 1984) and compliment responses in everyday discourse (Danziger, 2018), as well as public speech acts such as compliments and praise (Kampf & Danziger, 2019); apologies (Abadi, 1991; Kampf, 2009); and congratulations and good wishes (Kampf, 2016). Several of these studies connect the pragmatic patterns identified in speech act use to the Israeli communicative ethos of *dugri*, a speaking style that originated from the first settlers (known as *tsabarim*),[6] who valued directness, honesty, assertiveness, naturalness, solidarity, communitas, and "anti-style" (actions speak louder than words) (Katriel, 1986). This communication ethos dictates an unembellished and straightforward speaking style that aims to maintain solidarity – for example, a tendency toward directness in requests, mitigated by frequent use of nicknames (Blum-Kulka, 1990, [1992] 2005; Blum-Kulka & Katriel, 1991). In an example from the latter study, an Israeli mother asks her daughter, Hagit, to put spoons (kapot, כפות in Hebrew) on the dinner table:

הגיתוש, כפות, חביתוש

Ḥagit-ush, kap-ot, Ḥavit-ush

Proper name-nickname suffix, spoon-pl.f, barrel[7]-nickname suffix

The mother only says the object of her request (spoons) without any "embellishments" such as "please," "would you," "could you," and other conventional negative politeness strategies (Brown & Levinson, 1987) common among Jewish American English speakers. Her very direct request is mitigated by the use of highly affectionate and idiosyncratic nicknames.

Since the 1980s, an erosion of the *dugri* style, parallel with the emergence of two related speaking styles, *kasaḥ* and *firgun*, has been documented. *Kasaḥ* (כסאח) refers to hostile, bashing talk that maintains the assertive directness of *dugri* without its infrastructure of solidarity. *Firgun* (פרגון), in contrast, is an interpersonal speaking style that maintains sincerity and solidarity in a competitive, individualistic environment (Katriel, 1993; Maschler, 2001; Dori-Hacohen, 2016; Danziger, 2018). Originating from the Yiddish פארגינען (farginen), "not to begrudge," the Hebrew verb *le-fargen* (לפרגן) roughly means "to give others a chance, not to judge them harshly, not to envy their success, and to support them both verbally and non-verbally" (Katriel, 1993: 31). The use of *firgun* (here in noun form) began in the late 1960s and caught on more in the 1980s, but its cultural importance was solidified in the 1990s. The most common example Israelis give for *firgun* is openly and genuinely supporting a coworker when they are promoted at work. This common example denotes an ideal social climate, known as *'ayirah mefargenet* (a supportive environment, אווירה מפרגנת) that aspires to reduce competitive tension by encouraging support and positive feelings (Katriel, 1993). Such an environment enables competition

---

[6] *Tsabarim* (צברים), literally "prickly pears," the common nickname of these early settlers and a synonym for native-born Israelis to this day.

[7] The word for "barrel" in Hebrew, ḥavit, rhymes with the girl's name, Hagit, which adds playfulness to the already affectionate nickname.

without competitiveness, which ideally preserves solidarity between equals. This conceptualization of social relations allows Israeli society to keep its *dugri* values of sincerity and solidarity by extending them to include new capitalistic values of competition and individualism that became more dominant in the 1980s, as a result of Americanization (First & Avraham, 2009).

Firgun as a communication ethos has become the prism through which the Hebrew-speaking community understands and enacts its positive communication speaking style (Danziger, 2018). Not only has it drawn the attention of scholars seeking to study Israeli society but it is also a common, everyday category used by speakers. As evidence, a search of the natural Hebrew language web corpus on Sketch Engine resulted in 13,874 items of *firgun*, which means it was mentioned more frequently than politeness (nimus, נימוס), which appears 11,546 times. Some items explicitly discuss *firgun* as a cultural ought, exchanging "love" with the imperative "*fargen*" in the "love thy neighbor" golden rule (*fargen leḥaverkha hayoshev leyadkha*, פרגן לחברך היושב לידך), invoking a great sense of reciprocity. Moreover, fourteen items described the importance and benefits of a supportive environment (*'ayirah mefargenet*), for example: "It feels so good to be part of a truly supportive [lit. *mefargenet*; ADJ] and nice community" (*ze na'ym kol kakh lihiyot ḥelek mekehilah mefargenet venehmadah*, זה נעים כל כך להיות חלק מקהילה מפרגנת ונחמדה). In this example from wordpress.com, the speaker mentions the positive feeling one gets from being part of a community that practices *firgun*. The amount and nature of this data demonstrate that the academic perception of *firgun* as a communication keyword and social ideal for a culture-specific understanding of positive communication and a "supportive environment" continue to be prevalent and fundamental in Israeli society.

3.2 Positive Social Actions under the Umbrella Term *"Firgun"*

Hebrew is a Semitic language that joins consonant roots with verb or noun derivation patterns of vowels (*binyan* and *mishkal*, respectively). Hebrew also allocates gender to both nouns and verbs. *Firgun* is a noun (SG.M), but it also conjugates as a verb, with the infinitive *le-fargen* (/le/ functions as /to/ does in English infinitives, like to run, to jump, to smile). Whenever an example is given in this section, the translation of *firgun*, a cultural keyword that does not have an English equivalent, will appear alongside its literal translation and a gloss of its conjugation.[8] For example, the conjugation of past tense in singular

---

[8] Glosses follow the Leipzig Glossing Rules, available at www.eva.mpg.de/lingua/resources/glossing-rules.php (accessed July 22, 2022).

third person, male form is *firgen* (PST.3SG.M) and the imperative in singular second person, female form is *tefargeni* (IMP.2SG.F).

The 13,874 items of *firgun* were collected by searching all possible variations of the Hebrew root f.r.g.n (פ.ר.ג.נ), a total of 12 forms. Only 50 items of each form were collected into a sub-corpus (N = 600); 9 items were removed because they referred to the city Fargona (פרגונה) in Uzbekistan, which is homographic to one verb conjugation of *firgun* (*firgena*; PST.3SG.F). Additionally, 38 items were removed because they were identified as duplicates. A total of n = 553 items were analyzed for the social actions that were given the label of *firgun* and the metapragmatic comments that accompanied the evaluation.

The social actions that received the label of *firgun* in the corpus were various acts of support (either moral, emotional, or tangible support) (Example 1); praise and compliments (Example 2); recognition, appreciation, thanks, and gratitude (Example 3); recommendations (esp. places of business) (Example 4); good wishes (Example 5); congratulations (Example 6); giving someone the benefit of the doubt (Example 7); positive coverage in the media (Example 8); and acting generously (giving a gift or otherwise) (Example 9). Additional positive social actions were found less frequently and will therefore not be exemplified; these include reciprocity, help, constructive or mitigated criticism, portraying positivity, speaking positively about someone, acting kindly, being nice to someone, sugarcoating an unpleasant truth, and giving someone credit.[9] The following exemplifies the social actions that were given the label of *firgun* and why they were evaluated positively.

Support. The most frequent positive social action that received the label of *firgun* is supportive behavior in various forms. Showing support is not included in traditional taxonomies of expressive speech acts, but it includes an expression of positive feelings and solidarity that can manifest in various ways: empathizing with someone, identifying with the other's actions, expressing gratitude and appreciation (Kampf et al., 2019), stance-taking and aligning with other subjects (De Bois, 2007), laughing at someone's jokes (Hay, 2001), and much more. The following example is a post on a coaching website (dunetzcoaching.com), where a trainee thanked her coach for supporting her in a diet process:

1. תודה על ליווי צמוד הכולל מקצועיות, תמיכה, פרגון ובעיקר הקשבה והבנה ללא כל שיפוט

Todah 'al livuy tsamud hakolel miktzo'iyut, tmikhah, firgun vebe'ikar hakshavah ve havanah lelo' kol shiput

---

[9] Self-*firgun* is also possible. In this corpus, self-*firgun* is used to refer to self-love, self-care, and self-praise. This meaning is commonly harnessed by vendors to communicate something along the lines of "treat yourself, indulge or pamper yourself by buying our product."

> Thanks for accompanying [my process] so closely with such professionalism, support, *firgun* and mostly for listening and understanding without judgment

In Example 1, the speaker herself is performing a positive social action, namely giving thanks, using a "thank you" token followed by a detailed description of what is she is grateful for, that is, a previous supportive behavior from the addressee, her diet coach. Although, as a diet coach, the addressee is expected to provide support, when performing her thanks, the speaker is marking the coach's behavior as positive in a way that exceeded her expectations. Her expressions of gratitude for the positively marked social behavior demonstrate that it made her feel good, and so she is reciprocating with a thanks.

Praise. Praise and compliments and are expressive speech acts that have traditionally been seen as promoting solidarity and increasing commonality between speakers (Manes & Wolfson, 1981; Holmes, 1986; Jaworski, 1995). As solidarity-enhancing tools, they are unsurprisingly included under the umbrella term of *firgun* (Danziger, 2018; Kampf & Danziger, 2019). The following example was posted by a reader on a website promotion site called seori.co.il and addressed to the website administrator:

2. אורי היי קודם כל רציתי לפרגן לך על הפוסט הזה באמת עשית עבודה יפה פוסט ארוך וגם
איכותי אני למדתי ממנו הרבה

'ori hai kodem kol ratsiti lefargen lekha 'al hapost hazeh be'emet 'asita 'avodah yafah post 'arokh vegam 'ekhuti 'ani lamadeti mimeno harbeh

Ori Hi first of all I wanted to praise [lit. *le-fargen*; INF] you for this post you really did a beautiful job a long post and also [in good] quality I learned a lot from it.

In Example 2, the speaker is publicly praising Ori, the writer of the blogpost, on his work ("you really did a beautiful job") while labeling this positive evaluation as *firgun*. His *firgun* is strengthened by emphasizing the speaker's perspective ("I wanted"; "I learned") and the addition of intensifiers ("really," "a lot," "beautiful"). Thus, providing a positive evaluation of another can be seen as a way to show support and enhance the other's face.

Thanking Someone. Thanking someone is an expressive speech act that often functions as a device to promote sociability, by balancing obligations (Ohashi, 2008), enhancing solidarity (Eisenstein & Bodman, 1993), and maintaining a polite and friendly atmosphere (Leech, 1983). Example 3 was posted on opendoor.org.il, the website of a nonprofit organization that promotes healthy sexuality. It was written by a relationship and sexuality expert for youth who provides advice on how to improve a relationship by expressing *firgun*, in the form of gratitude.

3. בדרך כלל אנחנו לא אומרים לא (*לו) מה כן עושה לנו טוב, אלא רק מה לא, ואז מתקבל הרושם כאילו כל מה שקורה הוא לא תמיד מוצלח. אני הייתי מציעה לך לפרגן לו על כל מחווה הכי קטנה שהוא עושה, פותח דלת, מזמין אותך במסעדה, צימר, להגיד לו המון תודה על כל מה שהוא עושה ולתת לו מוטיבציה.

bederekh klal 'anaḥnu lo' 'omrim lo' (sic, *lo) ma ken 'oseh lanu tov, 'el'a rak mah lo', ve'az mitkabel haroshem keilu kol mah shekoreh ho lo' tamid mutslaḥ. 'ani hayiti matsi'a lakh lefargen lo 'al kol maḥvah hakhi ktana shehu 'ose, poteaḥ delet, mazmin otakh bemis'adah, tsimer, lehagid lo hamon todah 'al kol mah shehu 'ose velatet lo motivatsyah.

We usually don't tell him what does make us feel good, only what doesn't, and then it gives the impression that everything that happens is not always good. I would suggest that you show him gratitude [lit. *le-fargen*; INF] even for the smallest gesture [like] opening the door [for you], getting the bill in a restaurant, a [night at a B&B], say thank you a lot for everything he does and motivate him.

The expert claims that expressing *firgun* through gratitude motivates the recipient to perhaps repeat the positive actions that earned an expression of gratitude or to advance the relationship. In this context, labeling gratitude as *firgun* implies that a positively marked action has been performed and is perceived as such by the speaker (Wierzbicka, 1987).

Recommendation. A public recommendation to potential consumers is a form of support for a store because it can increase sales and profitability and enhance the store's reputation (Willemsen et al., 2011). It is also a way to perform a positive action toward others in the community – in other words, direct them toward a product that will make them feel good. Example 4 is a review on a baby store website called pomfitis.com:

4. אני ממליצה בחום בפורומים שאני פעילה ולכל הורה שאני מכירה!! אם אני מתלהבת ממוצר, אני מפרגנת עד הסוף. בבוא העת, ננסה את המוצרים האחרים לאמבטיה

'ani mamlitsah beḥom beforumim she'ani pe'ilah velekol horeh she'ani makirah!! 'im 'ani mitlahevet mimutsar, 'ani mefargenet 'ad hasof. bevo' ha'et, nenase et hamutsarim ha'aḥrim la'ambatyah.

I warmly recommend [the products I like] on online forums and to every parent I know!! If I like a product, I show wholehearted support [lit. *mefargenet*; PRS.1SG.F]. In time, we'll try the other bathtub products.

In this positive public review, the speaker is attempting to enhance the reputation of the store (a form of face enhancement). The speaker is reinforcing her *firgun* by using intensifiers ("warmly," "every," "wholehearted") that indicate sincerity. This is not a dyadic form of *firgun* per se; it is more a social action that promotes solidarity in the community.

Good Wishes. Good wishes are expressive speech acts that express hope that a gladdening event will happen to the addressee in the future (Kampf et al., 2019). They have been shown to maintain, affirm, and reestablish good relationships by communicating involvement and concern (e.g., Dumitrescu, 2006; Kampf, 2016). Example 5 is from a personal blog at noaasworld.com. The blogger has written a post after leaving her workplace in which she explains why she left and that it was not because of her colleagues, whom she loved:

5. אני אהבתי ואוהבת את האנשים שעבדתי איתם ואני מפרגנת להם הרבה הצלחה בהמשך

'ani 'ahavti ve'ohevet 'et ha'anashim she'avadeti 'itam ve'ani mefargenet lahem harbeh hatslaḥah bahemshekh

I liked and still like the people I worked with, and I wish them [lit. *mefargenet*; PRS.1SG.F] plenty of success in the future

The speaker has given an update on her personal blog about leaving a workplace amicably, saying that despite having left the workplace, she does not hold a grudge against her coworkers; on the contrary, according to her words, she is showing *firgun*, that is, wishing them all the best. By engaging in the positive action of good wishes, she is perhaps avoiding conflict or relationship deterioration (Holmes & Marra, 2004).

Congratulations. Congratulations are an expressive speech act that promotes solidarity by signaling pleasure in light of a gladdening event that happened in the past (Kampf, 2016) or by expressing pleasure at the good fortune of the hearer (Searle & Vandervaken, 1985). Example 6 is a news report on an Israeli sports website, walla.co.il, that presents a famous football player's reaction to a recent tournament achievement:

6. גם ויקטור ואלדס פרגן וצייץ: "מברך את הנבחרת הצעירה על זכיה באליפות אירופה. אתם גדולים!"

gam viktor valdes firgen vetsiyets: "mevarekh 'et hanivḥeret hatse'irah 'al zkhiyah be'alifut 'eropah. 'atem gdolim!"

Victor Valdes also supported [lit. *firgen*; PST.3SG.M] and tweeted: "I congratulate the [U-20 national Spanish team] for winning the European cup. You are awesome!"

The Israeli sports reporter interpreted the football player's speech act, or positive social action of congratulations, as *firgun*. By labeling the non-Israeli's words as *firgun*, the reporter is positively marking the congratulations as supportive.

Give Someone the Benefit of the Doubt. Katriel's (1993) definition of *firgun* includes "not to judge others harshly." Giving someone the benefit of the doubt is doing just that: not rushing to conclusions; giving the other person a chance despite being faced with evidence of falsehood. This is particularly notable if that person is a friend or loved one. We demonstrate "epistemic partiality" (Faulkner, 2018) toward people we care about because of trust and belief in that person. Giving someone the benefit of the doubt is a positive social action that potentially saves face and avoids unnecessary conflict. The speaker in Example 7 is giving advice on how to diffuse relational tension by giving the other side the benefit of the doubt.[10]

7. לשמוע קודם את הצד השני – מה יש לו לומר "להגנתו". ולחכות מעט. לא לומר באותו רגע. תפרגני, תדוני לכף זכות, תחכי, תנשמי, תראי שפתאום כבר לא בטוח שזה היה כ"כ נורא כמו שחשבת.

lishmoa' kodem 'et hatsad hasheni – ma yesh lo lomar "lehaganto". velehakot me'at. lo' lomar beoto rega'a. tefargeni, taduni lekaf zkhut, tehaki, tinshemi, tir'i shepit'om kvar lo batuah shezeh hayah k"k (kol kakh) nora' kmo shehashavt.

Listen to the other side first – what he has to "say for himself." And wait a little. Don't say anything in that moment. Give him the benefit of the doubt [lit. *tefargeni*; IMP.2SG.F], judge favorably, wait, breathe, you'll suddenly see that it might not be as bad as you thought.

It is interesting that giving someone the benefit of the doubt is nonaction; the speaker is advising to "wait" and "not say anything in that moment." Not acting or speaking entails the performance of supportive and friendly *firgun*.

Positive Coverage by the Media. The next example is from an interview with a well-known Israeli reporter, Hadas Shtaif, published in *Haaretz*, an Israeli daily. The long profile piece tells the narrative of a journalist who fights back and does not shy away from controversy. When she explains why she left the newspaper *Israel Hayom*, she says:

8. הסבירו לי שהעיתון רוצה דיווחים חיוביים ושהמדיניות היא לפרגן למפכ"ל (יוחנן דנינו), אז הבנתי שאין לי מה לעשות שם.

hesbiru li sheha'iton rotse divuhim hiyuviyim veshehamediniyut hi' lefar-gen lamafkal (yohanan danino), 'az hevanti she'en li ma la'asot sham.

I was told that the newspaper wanted positive reports and that the policy is to cover [the work of] the Chief of Police (Johanan Denino) in a positive way [lit. *le-fargen*; INF], so I realized I don't belong there.

Media coverage is expected to be as impartial as possible, while challenging power. Providing a positive coverage to a public figure as a policy is the

---

[10] From mabtim.com; no longer available.

opposite of what is expected of journalism. In Example 8, undeserved and perhaps coerced positive coverage by the media is labeled *firgun*. Contrary to specific positive social actions considered *firgun*, in this case *firgun* refers to journalistic policy dictated by a certain newspaper. This example elaborates on the traditional definition of *firgun* to include *insincere* positive support resulting from the demands of powerful actors in the political world. The use of *firgun* in this example may be euphemistic because the positive social action of positive coverage functions as an appeasement or bribe of sorts.

Acting Generously. Acting generously means to show a willingness to give money, help, kindness, and so on, especially more than is usual or expected.[11] Therefore, it is a positive social act that will often be positively marked. Example 9 is from a personal blog on blogspot.co.il written by a Hebrew speaker staying in Japan:

9. הזמנתי קולה, בעיקר כי אני אוהבת קולה ואני בקושי שותה אותה מאז שהגעתי ליפן. גם חברתי הזמינה קולה. כבונוס נוסף, הוא גם פירגן עם הרוטב והמיונז על האוקונומיאקי שהזמנתי.

> hezmanti kolah, be'ikar ki 'ni 'ohevet kolah ve'ani bekoshi shotah 'otah me'az shehega'ati leyapan. gam ḥaverti hezmina kolah. Kebonus nosaf, hu' gam firgen 'im harotev vehamayonez al ha'okonomiyaki shehezmanti.

> I ordered a coke, mostly because I like coke and I barely drink it since I came to Japan. My friend ordered a coke as well. As an extra bonus, [the waiter] gave us extra [lit. *firgen*; PST.3SG.M] sauce and mayonnaise for the okonomiyaki I ordered

The action framed as *firgun* in this example is a waiter giving extra condiments in a restaurant, more than he is required to do. The Hebrew speaker interpreted the non-Israeli's act of generosity as *firgun*. From the text alone, it is not possible to know whether the speaker verbally acknowledged the waiter's gesture. However, from her use of the label *firgun* we can deduce that she at least perceived it as positively exceeding her expectations. This example of a positive social action is even further away from the conventional definition of *firgun* (Katriel, 1993). It shows *firgun* has expanded to also mean "give generously," when receivers feel something has been done in their favor, positively exceeding their expectations.

Owing to limitations of length, this list of examples only includes nine of the most common kinds of positive social action that received the metapragmatic

---

[11] See the definition of "generously" in the *Cambridge Dictionary*, Cambridge Dictionaries Online website (https://dictionary.cambridge.org/dictionary/english/generously) (accessed March 3, 2022).

label of *firgun*. It nonetheless shows that this label has grown significantly to cover a fairly large variety of behaviors that are built on the premise of support, such as praise, congratulations, and giving thanks, to name a few. This adds to the original definition of *firgun* that described it as showing verbal and nonverbal support, giving others a chance, and not begrudging them or envying their success (Katriel, 1993). The examples in this section demonstrate the gamut of possible linguistic resources that can be used to promote sociability. As argued in Section 2, social acts are not limited to expressive speech acts; they can also be conventional positive politeness strategies and various social actions that express friendliness, solidarity, or reciprocity, all other-oriented positive social actions that are aimed at making the other feel good, enhancing face, or promoting sociability. They are all forms of positive communication that were seen as such, appropriate and frequently positively marked, and thus receive the metapragmatic label of *firgun*.

Examples in which Hebrew speakers judge the positive social actions of non-Israelis as *firgun* demonstrate that it is the prism through which they make sense of positive communication, despite the keyword being completely culture-specific. Hebrew speakers' frequent complaints about the general lack of *firgun* (Rosenblum & Triger, 2007) imply that *firgun* is culturally expected and, as a result, its absence is marked. The next example is from 4girls.co.il, an online community for young women:

10 אז פשוט תשני את הגישה שלך!! אולי תשמחי בשביל אח שלך שמצליח יפה?! אולי
תפרגני קצת? איזו קנאית!!

'az pashut teshani 'et hagishah shelakh!! 'ulay tiśmeḥi bishvil 'aḥ shelakh shematsliaḥ yafe?! 'ulay tefargeni ktsat? 'eizu kana'it!!

So just change your attitude!! How about being happy for your brother who is doing well? Maybe show some support? [lit. *tefargeni*; IMP.2SG. F] You are such a jealous person!

Example 10 is a textbook case in which *firgun* is expected: a sister is being chastised for not displaying pleasure at her brother's success. Lack of support for the success of another is perceived as negatively marked behavior and socially unacceptable jealousy.

The specific cultural understanding of positive communication among Hebrew speakers in Israel is therefore anchored in the values of mutual support, communitas, reciprocity, and the general stance of sincere positive intentions toward the other. These values demonstrate, at least in regard to cultural expectations (not necessarily de facto), a continuation of the collectivist culture from the early days of Israeli society (Katz & Haas, 2001). It illustrates how individual acts are based on both personal and social preferences and expectations. Judging someone as supportive or not (*mefargen*; PTCP.M, or not) is based on a personal as well as collective evaluation. Followingly, I will delve into the collective aspect of interaction known in pragmatic literature as the moral order.

3.3 Positive Communication and the Moral Order: #FAMING

The Israeli nonprofit organization Good Deeds Day holds an annual good deeds day every March. In 2021, the organization launched a #FAMING campaign that encouraged the public to shine a spotlight on people doing good deeds and publicly praise them on social media. The idea of publicly praising the other's good deeds was designed to counter surging negativity in the public sphere with positivity. The concept is not exclusive to Israel; it appeared in the Urban Dictionary in March 2016 and it represents a shift from the concept of shaming.[12] Instead of naming and shaming to mark the deviators and maintain the moral order (Rowbottom, 2013), this new initiative proposes naming and faming those who are morally good and presenting them as role models in society.

The idea of public praising to counter or complement public shaming can be connected to Aristotle's epideictic rhetoric, the language of public praise and blame that sets models of civic behavior in a specific society (Beale, 1978; Hauser, 1999). In pragmatics, this model is commonly referred to as the moral order. A moral order is a culture-specific ideology relating to what counts as right or wrong (Culpeper & Tantucci, 2021: 148). Publicly praising a community member's good deeds not only maintains the social order but also indicates what values the community upholds most dearly. In the Hebrew-speaking community in Israel, the discourse around faming is heavily anchored in the more widespread and fundamental idea of *firgun*. Example 11 is from eol.co.il, the website of Essence of Life, an organization that seeks to "raise awareness and provide tools for inner peace." It discusses faming and why we should all practice it:

11. אז הרעיון הוא לפרגן ולפרסם את הדברים הטובים שסביבנו: לשלוף את המצלמה כשאנו רואים מישהו עוזר לאדם מבוגר לסחוב את הקניות, באותה מהירות שאנו שולפים אותה כשאנו עדים להתקוטטות; לכתוב שבחים על הפקיד שעזר לנו באותו להט שאנו כותבים נגד חברת האינטרנט שתסכלה אותנו. הקרדיט לאחרים, מעבר לכך שהוא מגיע להם, עוזר גם לנו בכך שהוא מאלץ אותנו לראות את המציאות בצורה מאוזנת יותר

'az hara'ayon hu' lefargen velefarsem 'et hadvarim hatovim shesvivenu: lishlof 'et hamatslemah kshe'anu ro'im mishehu 'ozer le'adam mevugar lishov 'et hakniyot, be'otah mehirut she'anu sholfim 'otah kshe'anu 'edim lehitkotetut: likhtov shvahim 'al hapakid she'azar lanu be'oto lahat

---

[12] "Faming," Urban Dictionary website (www.urbandictionary.com/define.php?term=Faming) (accessed July 19, 2021).

she'anu kotvim neged ḥevrat ha'internet shetiskelah 'otanu. Hakredit le'aḥerim, me'ever lekakh shehu' magi'a lahem, 'ozer gam lanu bekakh shehu' me'alets 'otanu litr'ot 'et hametsi'ut betsurah me'uzenet yoter

So the idea is to [perform] *firgun* [lit. *le-fargen*; INF] and advertise the good things all around us: to pull out [our] camera when we see someone helping an elderly man carry the groceries, as fast as we would if we witnessed a fight; publicly praise the clerk who helped us, as passionately as we would post our frustrations with the internet supplier. Giving others credit when credit is due, also helps us by compelling us to see life in a more balanced way

It encourages publicly acknowledging people for their performance of the positive social act of helping those in need. These virtuous people are to be rewarded with public fame. As the post demonstrates, the idea behind the campaign is simple: actually do (not just expect it) what the moral order in the Hebrew-speaking community dictates, that is, create an atmosphere of solidarity by performing *firgun*, especially by publicly praising those who deserve it. The connection between faming and *firgun* reveals the importance of practicing *firgun* and the potential consequences of positive communication for members of a community, both for the individual and at the collective level. Giving faming a localized or emic metapragmatic label indicates that positive communication is both highly valued and expected in the Hebrew-speaking community (even though at times it is not practiced enough). The shared set of norms and ethos regarding the performance of public discourse that takes us to the collective level of politeness in a democratic community is known as (in)civility (Sifianou, 2019).

3.3.1 (In)civility

(In)civility scholarship has traditionally put its emphasis on incivility – for example, the uncivil public or political discourse among members of a democratic society (Papacharissi, 2004; Mutz & Reeves, 2005; Brooks & Geer, 2007; Jamieson et al., 2017). (Im)politeness and (in)civility are two levels of the same social norms regarding communication and discourse. Politeness describes the interpersonal level and civility describes the public or collective level. Civility therefore "is a social norm and a standard of behavior ... based in widely shared beliefs [about] how individual group members ought to behave in a given situation" (Feher & Fischbacher, 2004: 185). Civility differs from moral order in that the former refers to the norms of a democratic society, while the latter refers to the culture-specific ideology about what counts as right or wrong in any given society. Politeness, civility, and the moral order are coexisting concepts that describe different (yet sometimes overlapping) aspects of social interaction. As a label for socially approved positive communication, *firgun* can be seen as part of the moral order according to which judgments of politeness and civility are made in Israeli culture. The next section will discuss the relation between positive communication and politeness in light of culture-specific perceptions of positive social actions.

3.4 Positively Evaluated Communication: *Firgun* vs. Politeness

While the concept of politeness is universal, every culture has an emic understanding of what politeness is. Emic concepts are "culture-specific resources in the form of concepts and terms … a set of understandings and descriptive practices by which [members] index aspects of what they are doing" (Arundale, 2013: 113). Some cultures such as Greek (Sifianou, 1992), Polish (Ogiermann, 2015), Turkish (Ruhi & Işık-Güler, 2007), and English-speaking communities in Australia and New Zealand (Haugh, 2019), see consideration as the central value that leads evaluations of politeness, while others, such as the Japanese (Fukushima, 2009) and Chinese (Chang & Fukushima, 2017) cultures, point to attentiveness. Consideration as the value leading evaluations of politeness means that members of these linguacultures will expect an utterance to show care or concern for the other interlocutor in order to be judged as polite (Sifianou, 1992; Haugh, 2019). Attentiveness is considered a type of consideration that is better explained in terms of the heart rather than face because it is motivated by empathy, altruism, and helping behaviors (Fukushima, 2019).

In an attempt to study the culture-specific elements of Israeli politeness, Blum-Kulka ([1992] 2005) asked Hebrew speakers to define politeness (more specifically, what Locher and Watts [2005] would consider politeness1, that is, what participants in an interaction mean when *they* use the term "polite"). Participants provided two main connotative definitions: a positive one that included patience and tolerance, restraint, courtesy, respect, and kindness; and a negative one, which perceived politeness as external, dishonest, and unnatural. These lay definitions demonstrate a conflation of positive and polite communication, giving examples of both behaviors and evaluations. They also resemble the Western folk tradition of decorum but come with the cultural warning that politeness is the external packaging of communication that serves as a means to avoid harming face. Like Blum-Kulka ([1992] 2005), Katriel (1991) notes that Israelis demonstrate ambivalence toward politeness: on the one hand, they are aware that politeness expresses consideration and maintains harmony; on the other, due to the first settlers' (*tsabars*) perception of politeness as artificial, they may see it as a façade or a diplomatic way to get something. She later suggests that Israelis perceive *firgun* and politeness as mutually exclusive because politeness is seen as an obligatory or social convention, as opposed to the genuine, sincere, and volitional action of *firgun* (Katriel, 1993). Since *firgun* has become the keyword for positive communication in the Hebrew-speaking society in Israel, I would like to suggest that *firgun* is the emic concept underlying positive communication in Israeli culture and that sincere support is the main value in the Israeli moral order that dictates the production and evaluation of positive social actions.

Since sincere interactional support is the main value of *firgun*, the notion of reciprocity is understandably salient in the examples discussed in this section. The expectation of the performance of *firgun* (in any of the relevant positive social acts) at the collective social and interpersonal levels, combined with the "supportive environment" (*avira mefargenet*) ideal and values of support and solidarity, can all stem from the principle of reciprocity. Culpeper and Tantucci (2021: 161) recently formulated the principle of (im)politeness reciprocity, as a socio-pragmatic interactional principle closely related to the moral order, stating that it is

> a constraint on human interaction such that there is pressure to match the perceived or anticipated (im)politeness of other participants, thereby maintaining a balance of payments.

Reciprocating positive action with positive action is therefore expected and its performance can be positively marked. It follows then that matching positive with positive can advance sociability. An illustrative example can be seen in the pressure to reciprocate and maintain a credit–debit balance in Japanese culture (Ohashi, 2008). In the linguistic ritual of o-rei, gratitude phone calls are made in order to symbolically rebalance relationships after gift-giving events. Ohashi describes reciprocity as fundamental in Japanese culture, stating that it is not meant to "clear a debt" but to maintain a delicate balance that ensures a continuation of the relationship. A perfect balance would mean undoing the social tie in question, because an equilibrium means interactants are free from the bond. Here, the importance of reciprocity to the maintenance of sociability is quite clear, and it too functions on both a social and an interpersonal level. Culpeper and Tantucci (2021) suggest that reciprocity is universal, but the specific ways a culture will interpret the principle of reciprocity and how it comes into play in its positive communication style are an interesting path to pursue in the future.

3.5 Summary

This section explored the "bright" side of sociability, that is, positive social actions that are evaluated as appropriate, polite, and acceptable and therefore can potentially achieve sociability. In this section, we have seen examples of how the metapragmatic label of *firgun* is used to mark positive social actions of others, or how it is used by speakers to frame their actions as positive on both the individual and the collective level. Analysis has revealed the positive social actions that fall under the umbrella term for positive communication in the Hebrew-speaking community: expressive speech acts such as praise, compliments, congratulations, good wishes, and giving thanks, as well as various acts of support, generosity, reciprocity, and solidarity. We have also seen how the emic understanding of faming as a type of *firgun* indicates that the pragmatic moral order of Hebrew speakers is founded on sincere support and reciprocity. The use of the keyword implies an active promotion of solidarity by adhering to the moral order expected in the community regarding positive communication. Culture-specific understanding of positive communication is part of the moral order and therefore forms the basis for politeness and civility evaluations. Positive communication is evaluated as appropriate when it meets or positively exceeds expectations on both the individual and the collective level. Thus, actors will judge the performance of text (the social actions) in context (Is it expected?) and based on culture (What does the specific moral order dictate regarding use of positive communication?). Having established what is positively marked positive communication, I will move on to consider negatively marked positive communication in the next section.

4 Negatively Evaluated Positive Social Acts: Over-Politeness

In Section 3, we saw instances in which positive communication is positively evaluated, that is, when positive social actions are deemed appropriate, expected, or positively exceeding expectations with regard to text, context, and sociocultural norms. However, there are also instances where positive social actions negatively exceed expectations. If we revisit the example of positively evaluated positive social actions from Section 3, in which someone approaches us to praise us for the presentation we have just given, that performance of a positive act can negatively exceed our expectations. If, for example, the praise is exaggerated, or too good to be true, we might think that person is being hyperbolic. If the person who praised us speaks a different language from that in which the praise is performed, we may suspect the inappropriate use of language stems from a cultural difference in pragmatic norms. Lastly, we may also suspect that the person needs something from us. Crossing the line from appropriateness to inappropriateness was termed over-politeness by Locher and Watts (Watts, 2003; Locher, 2004; Locher & Watts, 2005) because they saw it as an excess of politeness – that is, negatively marked, non-politic, or inappropriate within the context.

Over-politeness has not received much scholarly attention. Exceptions include Culpeper (2008, 2011), Izadi (2016), Danziger (2020), and Danziger and Kampf (2021), all of which offer additional theoretical developments as well as empirical explorations of over-politeness. In Culpeper (2008, 2011), impoliteness is at the center of the studies, while over-politeness is addressed as related negatively marked/inappropriate behavior. Culpeper elaborates on Locher and Watts' distinction between appropriateness and markedness, stating that while these are different concepts, they should be treated as scales of "normal" to "creative" use of language. Expectations about appropriacy in context are based on two different kinds of norms, experiential and social, which can lead to different evaluations of behavior. Lastly, Culpeper remarks that behavior receiving the label of over-politeness is not always interpreted negatively.

A case in point is interpretations of positive social acts as flattery by Hebrew speakers. In Danziger (2020), I have shown that flattery is a metapragmatic label given to solidarity-oriented actions that are evaluated as strategic, manipulative, or instrumental. As such, flattery is not a conventionalized speech act but a label for positive social acts that exceeded expectations in context. Judging an action as flattery involves the assessment of textual cues and contextual clues (Weizman & Dascal, 1991) filtered through culture- and society-specific meanings attributed to the action. Flattery is therefore an evaluative product of meaning-making processes. Various positive social acts can receive the label of flattery, among them the unsurprising speech act of compliments and praise but also thanks, apologies, and congratulations. The label of flattery is given not only to speech acts but also to other behaviors and actions that abuse the positive effect expected from positive social acts such as terms of endearment, nicknames, and expressions of love and care. Though flattery is an evaluative label for inappropriate use of positive social acts (or in politeness1 terms, manipulative use), Hebrew speakers will consider behaviors they have labeled flattery as positive when they do not cause face damage.

In Danziger and Kampf (2021), we compared judgments of positive social acts as flattery by Hebrew and Arabic speakers in Israel. Izadi (2016) studied examples of positive social acts being given the label of over-politeness in Persian culture, in a specific context of academic life. Both studies demonstrate how cultural communication styles interact with judgments of over-politeness. More specifically, they show that the line between appropriateness and inappropriateness is crossed at different points across the specific relational work continuum in each culture. I will return to and expand on this point in Section 4.2, but first, this is a good point to address the issue of language-specific labels. In Hebrew, flattery, ingratiation, and adulation all translate to the same word – *ḥanupa*. In Danziger and Kampf (2021), we noted that 57 percent of the Hebrew speakers in our study expressed a negative stance toward the Hebrew equivalent *ḥanupa* (חנופה), compared to 92 percent of the Arabic speakers representing the literary Arabic equivalent *tamalluq* (تملق) with negative terms. It remains unknown for now what the stance toward the English term "flattery" is for English speakers. The possibility to say "you flatter me" in English, for example, as a modest and pleased response to a compliment, without the implication of a manipulative intent by the complimenter, may indicate that the English label "flattery" has a more positive connotation than its Hebrew or Arabic equivalents. The use of the term "flattery" in this Element is based on the pragmatic definition in Danziger (2020: 423), as

> a marked communicative action; [that] is intended to be face-pleasing to the recipient, an effect that mediates one of three interactional goals of the flatterer: transactional, self-promotional, or relational. The action is perceived by at least one participant in an interaction as instrumental after evaluating textual cues and contextual clues.

In social psychology research, the term sometimes used for this phenomenon of strategic use of positive social acts for the benefit of the speaker is "ingratiation" (e.g., Jones, 1964). The choice to use the term "flattery" here and elsewhere is due to its mention in pragmatic works on manipulative intents and compliments in danger of being perceived as *flattery* (e.g., Barnlund & Araki, 1985; Holmes, 1986; Lewandowska-Tomaszczyk, 1989).

Seeing manipulative intent as an indication that a compliment is "actually" flattery demonstrates the conflation of positive and polite communication in pragmatic literature mentioned in Section 2. The discussion in Section 2 showed that over-politeness is a negative evaluation of positive social actions and the crossing from appropriateness to inappropriateness. By distinguishing between positive communication and polite communication, we can see more clearly that what the speaker actually intended to do or say with their words matters less than how their words were evaluated by hearers in that specific context. If a speaker performs a compliment with the purpose of advancing sociability but sociability is not achieved, then intention is not enough for a positive social act to succeed. However, interactants still interpret the actions of speakers and evaluate what they must have meant to do in their performance. This section will expand on this point and demonstrate how positive social actions are labeled over-politeness despite a speaker's intention.

4.1 Intention and Politeness

As the object of analytical study, the concept of intention is challenging. While classic pragmatic works on intention suggest it resides solely within the speaker (e.g., Searle, 1976), scholars from the sociocultural–interactional faction of pragmatics have more recently argued that intention is better understood as a "*post facto* participant resource" (Haugh, 2008a: 2). As a shared pragmatic resource, intention is negotiated discursively by participants, against the context of social and cultural norms evoked in an interaction (Haugh, 2008b). As a cognitive resource, intention is analytically beyond the scope of pragmatics. Haugh (2008a) proposes the notion of accountability to fill this gap, because when a speaker is held accountable for the implications of their words, it is possible to approach intention empirically.[13] A case in point, described by Haugh, regards a comment made by the Mufti of Australia in a sermon in a mosque in Sydney; the Mufti compared women who dress immodestly to "uncovered meat" that attracts flies. The comment made headlines because nonmembers of the group interpreted it as offensive to women (i.e., victim blaming), while the Mufti himself (or people speaking on his behalf) explained that this comment was not intended to be offensive, and it would not be evaluated as such by its intended audience in the context in which it was made. Those who held the Mufti accountable for the implied intention of his comment claimed that whether he meant to be offensive or not is irrelevant because, once they are made public, words and intentions, especially those of a public figure, are open to interpretation. Hearers will interpret what was said according to how they perceive the intended meaning. This uptake, or negative evaluation of the Mufti's words by members of the Australian society, allowed scholars of pragmatics to analyze the hearers' interpretation of what was said.

Discursive approaches to politeness have traditionally used the notion of "uptake" to study intention (e.g., Terkourafi, 2015). Without a discursive uptake, it is quite impossible to analyze the cognitive process through which participants decode meaning. In their study of "ordinary misunder- standings," Weizman and Blum-Kulka (1992) describe this challenge from the participants' point of view. They demonstrate that in non-negotiated misunderstandings the object of the misunderstanding remains covert and completely potential. Just like intention, nondiscursive objects, such as per- ceptions, effect, and evaluation, are analytically challenging for scholars as well as speakers. However, they are nonetheless important for pragmatic analysis. In the absence of a discursive uptake, metapragmatic labels for perceptions, interpretations, and evaluations are a fitting solution for this analytical challenge. Therefore, when behaviors are coded as positive behav- ior but receive a label of exceeding expectation, such as over-polite,

---

[13] Accountability does not have to be discursively negotiated. Interactants are held accountable for their words and actions without explicitly being asked to do so. If, for example, I call someone by the wrong name, I may apologize and correct myself even if the other person has said nothing.

ingratiating, or creepy, it is an indication that a positive act has been evaluated negatively. Culpeper (2008, 2011), for example, searched for the metapragmatic labels of "over-polite" and "too polite" in the English WebCorp and Danziger (2020) searched Sketch Engine for flattery, a specific over-polite behavior in Hebrew. However, not all over-polite behavior will receive a specific metapragmatic label. For example, if an addressee judges a compliment to be flattery, they may simply reply with an awkward "thanks" and not accuse the addressee of using flattery, which would be extremely face-threatening. While some of these nondiscursive instances may be analytically challenging, eliciting metapragmatic comments from interactants may make them accessible. But what are other metapragmatic labels of over-politeness? And how do speakers negatively mark positive social actions? To answer these questions, we should first outline the conventional and unconventional metapragmatic labels of over-politeness and examine the contexts in which we are likely to find them.

4.2 The Semantic-Pragmatic Field of Over-Politeness

Since over-politeness is an underexplored area in pragmatics, a good starting point would be to establish what behaviors potentially fall under this overarching label. Eligible candidates are common behaviors carrying a metapragmatic label of over-friendliness, such as schmoozing, ingratiation, obsequiousness, and servility. But before embarking on this semantic journey, it is important to note three points: First, this theoretical exercise is a conceptual exploration of over-politeness, and it does not include data-driven findings. After conceptualization, events of over-politeness can be examined through empirical studies. Second, the association between being friendly and being polite is culture-specific to American and British English (Culpeper, O'Driscoll, & Hardaker, 2019) in contrast to the Japanese language, for example, in which politeness and friendliness are discrete concepts (Ide et al., 1992). This brings me to the third caveat of this endeavor: Metapragmatic labels and particularly those that are evaluative in nature, like politeness, are not semantically parallel across languages (Haugh, 2016). Haugh has demonstrated, for example, that English "politeness" and Japanese *"teineina"* are merely conceptual overlaps, not equivalents. He explains the fundamental fuzzy alignment of words and concepts "while words are indexical to concepts, concepts do not inhere in words. That is, the "meanings" of named concepts are not limited to the use of a word, nor are concepts limited to that which can be named" (Haugh, 2016: 47).

His assertion calls for an emic description and understanding of politeness in the studied culture. In the context of the Hebrew-speaking linguaculture that is at the center of this Element, this observation is pertinent; searching for the Hebrew equivalents of "over-polite" or "too polite" (menumas miday, מנומס מידי), as Culpeper (2008, 2011) has used for English, yields meager results – a total of five items in the online Hebrew corpus on Sketch Engine. This is because this literal translation does not sound native. Moreover, the metaprag-matic label of "too polite" in Hebrew will most likely mean that someone should have been direct or aggressive, instead of being nice and polite. Saying "she is too polite" means she should put herself first and not worry about offending others. A case in point can be found on the website of the Teachers' Association in Israel, which offers a Q&A with an "early childhood expert" in education.[14] The question was submitted by a mother who was worried that her three-year-old daughter was being too "nice and polite" (neḥmada vemenumeset נחמדה ומנומסת) because she always "asks for permission" (תמיד שואלת אם אפשר להצטרף) (tamid sho'elet 'im 'fshar lehitstaref) instead of simply doing what she wants. The mother asked for the expert's help in teaching her child to "stand her ground, know how to offend at times and not always be on her best behavior, or try to please [others] all the time" (la'amod 'al shelah, lada'at laha'aliv gam ken lef'amim velo' tamid lehitnaheg hakhi tov sheyesh, lenasot leratsot kol hazman, לעמוד על שלה, לדעת להעליב גם כן לפעמים ולא תמיד להתנהג הכי טוב שיש, לנסות לרצות כל הזמן). The expert immediately understands: "nobody wants to raise a pushover [lit. *frayer*]"[15] (vebeneynu, mi rotseh legadel yaldah frayerit? ובנינו, מי רוצה לגדל ילדה פראיירית?).

This example demonstrates not only that metapragmatic labels vary across linguacultures (like "flattery" for example, as mentioned at the beginning of this section) but also that the actual behavior that will receive the label varies. Moreover, the line between acceptable and unacceptable positive social behav-ior crosses in different locations of the relational work continuum, across cultures. In Danziger and Kampf (2021), we have shown that what Hebrew speakers in Israel consider to be flattery does not completely overlap with what Palestinian Arabic speakers in Israel consider to be flattery. For Hebrew speakers, the strategic use of positive language became unacceptable when it was perceived as face-harming, while for Palestinian Arabic speakers, the

---

[14] See the original post on the Teachers' Association in Israel website at www.itu.cet.ac.il/-ילדה מנומסת-מדי/ (accessed April 21, 2021).

[15] Being too polite is associated with being a *"frayer"* (originally from the German *"freier"* but loaned into Hebrew from the Yiddish פרייער), which is commonly considered the worst thing someone can be in Israeli culture. A frayer is a naive idiot who follows the rules, whether the government law or the code of conduct. The word presupposes that following the rules is foolish, because people are inherently cunning and will take advantage of the frayer. (For the full post by the Israeli linguist Ruvik Rosenthal, published in 2014, see www.ruvik.co.il/-פרייערפינת/2014/עיון.aspx, accessed March 23, 2022.)

detection of self-interest in the deployment of positive communication was more likely to be deemed socially unacceptable (i.e., flattery). Therefore, in order to study over-politeness in a linguaculture, it is necessary to first identify the culture-specific metapragmatic terms that denote over-politeness and then explore what behaviors they entail. Lastly, as Haugh (2016) has shown, using English as a scientific metalanguage in pragmatics does not lend itself to studying evaluative concepts like politeness. Since this Element is written in English, leaping from the scientific metalanguage to the different language of data will require a lot of explanations. In order to address this challenge, in this subsection I will explore the semantic-pragmatic field of "over-politeness" that pertains to English alone. As this is a theoretical exercise, I will remain within the semantics of English using dictionary definitions of common labels of over-politeness.

In order to start exploring the semantic-pragmatic field of over-politeness, I chose the lexeme "obsequious," because it is the word used for Aristotle's vice of excess friendliness mentioned in Section 1. The adjective is defined as "too eager to praise or obey someone."[16] In this short definition, we can already note some elements of over-politeness: The first is the word "too," an indication of the negative evaluation of the praise as excessive in context. The second is the word "praise," referring to a social action that in the appropriate context has a positive effect. The third is the interpersonal aspect of being obsequious; it is a behavior toward "someone," that is, it is an inherently interactional (and evaluative) concept.

A search on WordNet 3.1 provided a synonymic relation between "obsequious" and "bootlicking," "fawning," "sycophantic," and "toadyish."[17] The *Cambridge Dictionary* additionally offers "servile" and "creep" and the verbs "to schmooze" and "to grovel." "Servile," also an adjective, is similarly defined: "too eager to serve and please someone else"; this definition includes the same elements highlighted for "obsequious": positive action evaluated by an interactant as excessive. The words "bootlicking," "toadying," "ingratiating," "flattering," and "schmoozing" all describe interpersonal behaviors using positive social actions (praise, talk informally, please, be polite and helpful, give attention) but additionally introduce the notions of power and insincerity. In Figure 1, the semantic similarities between the concepts are highlighted.

---

[16] For the definition of "obsequious," see *Cambridge Dictionary*, Cambridge Dictionaries Online website (https://dictionary.cambridge.org/us/dictionary/english/obsequious?q=obsequious) (accessed February 1, 2022).

[17] WordNet 3.1 available at http://wordnetweb.princeton.edu/perl/webwn (accessed February 14, 2022).

Bootlicker (adj): someone who praises or is extremely polite to a more powerful or rich person in a way that is not sincere, usually in order to get an advantage for themselves

Schmooze (V): to talk informally with someone, especially in a way that is not sincere or to win some advantage for yourself

Ingratiate (V): to make someone like you by praising or trying to please them

Flatter (V): praise someone in order to make them feel attractive or important, sometimes in a way that is not sincere

Toadying (N): a lot of praise and artificially pleasant behaviour towards someone in authority, in an effort to get some advantage

Creep (adj): someone who tries to make someone more important like them by being very polite and helpful in a way that is not sincere

Fawn (V): to give someone a lot of attention and praise in order to get that person's approval

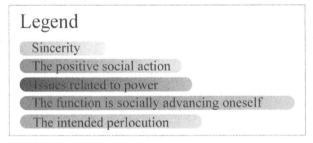

Legend
- Sincerity
- The positive social action
- Issues related to power
- The function is socially advancing oneself
- The intended perlocution

Figure 1 The semantics of English over-polite labels, according to the online *Cambridge Dictionary*.

As seen in Figure 2 and Table 1, "creep" is the lemma most commonly used in a web-based corpus. "Creep" is a polysemic word, especially in online discourse, where it may be used to denote additional behaviors that are not included in the *Cambridge Dictionary* definition. In the online Urban Dictionary, "creep" has five pages' worth of definitions, one of them being "A word used, usually as an insult, on someone who's personality or overall behaviour is strange or weird." Another says: "A man or woman who breaks social rules in an odd or obsessive way. Usually undesirable, clearly obsessed and somewhat pathetic."[18] Though not a formal dictionary, and even a dubious source at times, its lay definitions overlap with the *Cambridge Dictionary* definition in the semantic element of over-politeness as negatively exceeding expectations. The lemmas "toadying" and "bootlicking," on the other end, are absent from the corpus. Their absence helps us understand over-politeness as

---

[18] See "creep," Urban Dictionary website (www.urbandictionary.com/define.php?term=Creep) (accessed March 23, 2022).

Table 1 Over-politeness labels by frequency in English web corpus on Sketch Engine (by lemma, English arTenTen 2015).

Lemma	Frequency (absolute)	Frequency per million tokens
Creep	97777	6.34434
Fawn	17894	1.16107
Flattery	6267	0.40664
Servile	4277	0.27752
Grovel	4070	0.26409
Schmooze	2993	0.19420
Sycophantic	1547	0.10038
Obsequious	1520	0.09863
Toadying	0	0
Bootlicking	0	0

Figure 2 Over-politeness labels word cloud by frequency in the English web corpus Sketch Engine (by lemma, English arTenTen 2015).

a semantic field, but they are not necessarily used in everyday discourse. It is also important to note, once again, that these are merely dictionary definitions and may not fully correspond with how speakers actively use them. In Danziger (2020), for example, the pragmatic definition of "flattery" does not correspond with the dictionary definition that includes only the social action of praise, while empirical study has shown that flattery is an evaluative label and not a conventionalized speech act that can be given to a variety of positive social actions. That being said, what these definitions denote are friendly behaviors that somewhat exploit, for the benefit of the speaker, the positive effect expected from positive social actions. This discussion shows that conventional over-politeness labels cover socially coded norm violations or known behaviors that exceed acceptability of positive social actions use.

4.3 The Contexts of Over-Politeness

The previous section presented dictionary definitions for conventional English labels that exceed acceptability of positive social actions use, such as "ingratiation," "fawning," and "flattery," which exploit the positive effect expected from positive social acts for the benefit of the speaker. These are labels of over-politeness in that they denote conventional negative labels for positive-social-acts abuse. However, the instrumental exploitation of positive social actions is not the only context in which over-politeness occurs. Other over-politeness concepts like "too nice" or "too polite" are not in the dictionary; rather, they are everyday evaluations of language in context. Moreover, these concepts do not denote instrumental exploitations of positive social actions but the misuse of them. Judgment of positive social acts as over-polite, that is, exceeding contextual or textual expectations, can occur because of three reasons: failed politeness, intercultural pragmatic failure, and strategic use of positive communication. The next sections will describe and exemplify the three contexts that can give rise to evaluations of over-politeness. Unlike the systematic corpus-driven analysis of Section 3, this section is exploratory. It aims to discuss and describe the possible contexts in which we can find evaluations of over-politeness by analyzing illustrative examples. The examples in this section were either drawn from other studies of over-politeness or elicited ad hoc for the purpose of this Element. Consequently, the examples in this section are from several languages, namely Hebrew, Persian, Arabic, and English.

4.3.1 Failed Politeness

The first context is "failed politeness" (or "relational mismanagement"; Culpeper, 2008), that is, the speaker chooses a politeness strategy wrongly or their application of politeness is evaluated negatively by others within their speech community (Culpeper, 2011: 102). Judgments of over-politeness can derive from using positive social acts too frequently (e.g., saying thank you too much) or using hyperbolic or exaggerated language that exceeds the acceptable use of language in a specific context. The following example was originally collected for Danziger (2020), where I had used a diary method to elicit examples of flattery from Hebrew speakers. I had asked them to give an example of a time they flattered, were flattered, or witnessed flattery. The participant, an Israeli student who helped her friend with a class assignment, mentioned the exaggerated language her friend used as a marker for over-politeness:

12. , עזרתי לה בכל שאלה אבל היא הרגישה שהיא מציקה לי ולכן הגיבה לעזרה שלי בהודעות כמו "את המלכה שלי"

"bless your soul" (...) הרגשתי שהביטויים קצת מוגזמים ולכן הייתי קצת נבוכה, אבל ידעתי שבהקשר ועל פי מי שאמרה אותם הם כנים. לכן, הרגשתי גם שמחה על כך שמעריכים אותי

'azarti lah bekol she'elah 'aval hi' hegishah shehi' metsikah li velakhen hegivah la'ezrah sheli behoda'ot kmo "'at hamalkah sheli, bless your soul" (...) hergashti shehabituyim ktsat mugzamim velakhen haiyti ksat nevokhah, aval yad'ati shebaheksher ve'al pi mi she'amra 'otam hem kenim. Lakhen, hergashti gam śmeḥah 'al kakh shem'arikhim 'oti

I helped her with every question, but she felt like she was bothering me, so she responded to my help with messages [over WhatsApp] like "You're my queen" [or] "Bless your soul" (...) I felt that the expressions were a bit excessive and so I was a little embarrassed, but I knew by the context and the speaker that [the words] are sincere. So, I also felt happy about being appreciated.

Following the student's help, the friend was trying to reciprocate by showing gratitude, but her linguistic choices were "exaggerated," that is, inappropriate in relation to the expected performance of the positive social action in this context, to the point that the student felt "embarrassed." Thus, the positive effect the friend was going for slightly missed the mark. However, the recipient added that she knew her friend was being sincere and so she did feel appreciated. The relationship between the speakers was good and strong enough that the recipient could understand that this was a case of failed politeness, and while it made her uncomfortable, the gratitude still achieved the perlocutionary effect of feeling appreciated.

The positive effect described in Example 12 will not necessarily exist in any context of failed politeness. At times, the relationship between the speakers is a distant one. A relevant example can be found in Izadi (2016), which explored Persian over-politeness in the specific academic context of dissertation defenses in the English Language Teaching Department in an Iranian University. Izadi described the Persian culture's positive communication ethos of *Taarof*, "the language of politeness and praise ... a reciprocal exchange of ritualized (often exaggerated) honorifics that expresses good will and intentions and at times flattery and formalities" (Izadi, 2016: 14). One of the examples Izadi analyzed is a compliment response that is evaluated as over-politeness.

In the analyzed interaction, an examiner is performing an evaluation of the dissertation in question in the presence of the candidate and a supervisory team. This ritualistic speech event occurs completely in English, even though all the participants are Persian speakers. The evaluation traditionally includes a part for compliments and a part for criticism. When the examiner evaluated the dissertation positively, saying, "but the English was good," the candidate interrupts the examiner's monologue to respond to the compliment she has received, but not with a token acceptance or rejection, as expected (politic); rather, she produces a "hyperbolic" compliment return, saying, "I appreciate it hearing from you as a native speaker" (Izadi, 2016: 19). The examiner's uptake indicates she found this action to be inappropriate in context: She pauses, switches to Persian, and ritualistically rejects the compliment (as expected in Persian). She then switches back to English and adds "whatever." When the audience laughs, she switches back to Persian, saying she did not know how to respond to the candidate's *taarof*. Izadi concludes that this uptake indicates an evaluation of over-politeness. The examiner's code-switching may be another indication that she evaluated the candidate's compliment as the culture-specific *taarof* because it triggered a culture-specific response. Perhaps she chose to switch to Persian because she could not reconcile the different pragmatic norms of the two languages. This is an example of "relational mismanagement," in which the candidate did not adhere to the expected level of politeness in this context (a brief token acceptance or rejection of the compliment). She chose not only to return a compliment but to make it a clearly hyperbolic one, by calling the examiner, who is a Persian speaker, a "native English speaker." Her choice did not achieve its goal of pleasing the addressee; instead, it made the examiner uncomfortable – the latter evaluated the positive social actions as negatively exceeding expectations.

4.3.2 Intercultural Pragmatic Failures

The examples in the previous section are between speakers who are members of the same speech community and are therefore expected to know what the appropriate use of positive social acts in each context is. An evaluation of over-politeness in this context is an indication of a failure to do so by other participants in the interaction. However, judgments of over-politeness can arise in intercultural contexts, where participants in an interaction have diverging expectations of the appropriate use of positive social acts in context. Consequently, the second reason why positive social acts could be judged as over-polite is because of intercultural pragmatic failures (Thomas, 1983) or even ordinary misunderstandings stemming from undetectable clashes of social norms (Weizman & Blum-Kulka, 1992; Spencer-Oatey, 2008). As a lot of the literature suggests, the incorrect application of pragmatic strategies while speaking a foreign language can cause a pragmatic failure (e.g., Jaworski, 1994; Economidou-Kogetsidis, 2011; Isosävi, 2020). Jaworski (1994) reported on an intercultural pragmatic failure stemming from the intolerance of Polish students to the formulaic nature of the American English greeting of "How are you doing today?" The students interpreted it as a request for information, thus inappropriately answering a question instead of responding to a greeting.

Sometimes pragmatic failures can even occur between speakers of the same language. These cases are considered intercultural pragmatic failures in the sense that there is a clash between the social norms of the participants in the interaction. As such, the participants may speak the same language but have different expectations regarding the appropriate use of language in context. Microaggressions are a good example to illustrate this point. Microaggressions are instances of acts or remarks that make someone feel bad because of their race, sex, and so on, even though the act may have been unintended.[19] To illustrate, I will analyze a racist compliment in the public context of US politics. Complimenting presupposes that the thing the hearer is complimented for is good (Searle & Vanderveken, 1985). In this example, a compliment failed because of a different perception of what it considered "praiseworthy" (Holmes, 1986). The clash in social norms led to an unintended failure to achieve solidarity by complimenting.

The now infamous example of an attempt to compliment but failing miserably to do so happened in 2007 when then vice president Joe Biden described then president Barack Obama as the "first mainstream African-American who is articulate and bright and clean and a nice-looking guy."[20] Critical viewers read the implicature in Biden's linguistic choice of "first" as meaning that he thought other African Americans were neither "bright" nor "clean." Biden's attempt to compliment Obama failed because the other participants in the mediated interaction (observers, and possibly Obama himself) did not consider the traits mentioned to be praiseworthy. Biden later apologized and said he did not intend to cause offense to Obama. Here, we see an additional event where accountability steps in for intention: Holding a public figure accountable for the implication of his words makes his *actual* intention (or what he claims to have meant) irrelevant.

---

[19] See the definition of "microaggression" in the *Cambridge Dictionary*, Cambridge Dictionaries Online website (https://dictionary.cambridge.org/dictionary/english/microaggression) (accessed July 23, 2022).

[20] "Biden's description of Obama draws scrutiny," Politics report, CNN.com, February 9, 2007 (http://edition.cnn.com/2007/POLITICS/01/31/biden.obama/) (accessed February 1, 2021).

Not all pragmatic failures are cases of over-politeness. The examples given here may simply be failed speech acts, that is, speech acts that did not meet the required felicity conditions to achieve their desired perlocution. While a successful speech act meets the necessary felicity conditions and achieves the intended perlocution, achieving politeness is not a matter of felicity conditions but an evaluation of the language in context as appropriate. Therefore, failed politeness means a pragmatic strategy was evaluated negatively or inappropriate but not necessarily over-polite. This compliment was not evaluated as "too good" but as plain "racist."

However, an evaluation of over-politeness in intercultural contexts *can* be caused by an undetected pragmatic variation between speakers. What each culture perceives as over-politeness depends on the politeness norms of that speech community in a specific speech event. When an evaluation of over-politeness is made in a certain intercultural context, it will always be specific to the identity of the speakers in each conversational dyad. For example, a participant in Isosävi's (2020) study on (im)politeness norms of French and Finnish speakers who were cultural outsiders in their respective countries reported that the French greeting ritual, which includes kissing, is often evaluated as over-polite by Finnish speakers. Similarly, many Europeans, as well as Israelis, consider the friendly Anglo-American politeness style as "excessive" and "insincere" (Pinto, 2011).

The Anglo-American politeness style includes prevalent use of politeness tokens such as "please," "sorry," and "thank you," as well as linguistic formulae meant to maintain social harmony, such as "Have a nice day" and "We should get coffee sometimes" (Pinto, 2011). A few studies that compared the Anglo-American and the Israeli Hebrew politeness styles noted that Israelis are more direct than Anglo-Americans (Blum-Kulka, House, & Kasper, 1989; Blum-Kulka, 1990). Intercultural interactions between the two cultures have not been studied in pragmatic scholarship, but the common perception of Americans as very polite, on the verge of insincere, is nonetheless talked about in Israeli news blogs.[21]

The following examples come from young Israeli women who reported instances of over-politeness by American speakers of English when they were visiting the United States. I had contacted these women for the purpose of this Element, knowing they had extensive interaction with American English speakers. They are both native Hebrew speakers in their thirties. The speakers

---

[21] For examples, see H. Handwerker, "Lama 'amerikayim kol kakh menumasim?" [Why are Americans so polite?], Haaretz.co.il, October 17, 2017 (www.haaretz.co.il/blogs/haimhandwerker/BLOG-1.4494370) (accessed February 16, 2022);

N. Yehiely, "Lama ha'amerikayim lo' rotsim lihiyot ḥaverim sheli?" [Why don't Americans want to be my friends?], Mako.co.il, April 14, 2016 (www.mako.co.il/home-family-relationship/family-moving-america/Article-ef3679257101451006.htm) (accessed February 16, 2022).

produced these stories when I had asked them "can you recall an instance where Americans were being too polite [toward you] and you found it unpleasant or annoying?"[22] The following answer was a small story about getting lost in New Jersey and asking for directions:

13. פעם כשביקרתי את המשפחה שלי בניו ג'רזי הלכתי לאיבוד בדרך וביקשתי עזרה מאיזו משפחה, והם היו בעיקר עסוקים בלהתנצל שהם אוכלים מולי או לקרוא לי גברת (הייתי בת 14, כן?) ופחות בלהסביר לי איך אני מגיעה ליעד.

pa'am kshebikarti 'et hamishpaḥah sheli benyu jersy halakhti le'ibud baderekh vebikashti 'ezra me'eizu mishpaḥah, vehem hayu be'ikar 'asu-kim belehitnatsel shehem 'okhlim muli 'o likro' li geveret (hayiti bat 14, ken?) vepaḥot belehasbir li 'ekh 'ani magi'ah laya'ad.

I was going to visit my family in New Jersey, and I got lost on my way there [so] I asked some family [I saw] for help and [while they helped me] they were much more concerned with apologizing for eating in front of me or calling me Ms. (even though I was fourteen years old), and not concerned enough with explaining how I could reach my destination.

In Example 13, the Hebrew speaker found otherwise positive social actions (apology, honorific) as unnecessary and inappropriate; her expectation from this interaction was to be given what she had asked for, namely directions. The attempt by the family members to show their respect, in what could be considered negative politeness strategies in Brown and Levinson (1987) terms, was seen as counterproductive and completely irrelevant. This example reflects both the Israeli expectations of unembellished, direct speech and the common perception of American speech as excessive.

The next example is an answer from a young Israeli woman about a time she was working for a Jewish organization that organizes summer camps for Jewish children in the United States:

14. נסעתי הרבה לבתי כנסת ובתי ספר לעברית כדי לגייס חניכים ותרומות למחנה קיץ. ובאחד מבתי הספר קיבלתי כזו קבלת פנים שממש הרגשתי לא נוח, האישה שנפגשה איתי הייתה ממש נחמדה ומנומסת בצורה שהרגישה מזויפת ולא נעימה והתלהבה מכל מה שהיה לי להגיד למרות שידעתי שבעבר הם לא שיתפו פעולה עם [הארגון]. היא התעניינה בי בלי לשאול שום שאלה באמת אישית וזה הכל הרגיש כמו הצגה וזה פשוט היה מעצבן ומתסכל. לא התחייבה לכלום ובסוף זה היה בזבוז זמן.

nas'ati harbeh lebatey kneset vebatey sefer le'ivrit kedey legayes ḥanikhim vetrumot lemaḥaneh kayts. vebe'eḥad mibatey hasefer kibalti kazu kabalat

---

[22] The question was produced in Hebrew. The exact prompt was: היו אמריקאים שבו מקרה זוכרות אתן" "?בסגנון משהו או ?עצבן או נעים היה לא וזה אליכן מנומסים מידי יותר ('aten zokhrot mikre shebo 'amerikaym hayu yoter miday menumasim 'eleykhen veze haya lo na'im 'o 'izben? 'o mashu basignon?").

panim shemamash hergashti lo' noaḥ, ha'ishah shenifgeshah 'iti hayta mamash neḥmada vemenumeset betsurah shehergishah mezuyefet velo' ne'imah vehitlahava mikol ma shehayah li lehagid lamrot sheyad'ati sheba'avar hem lo shitfu pe'ula 'im [ha'irgun]. hi' hit'anyenah bi bli lish'ol shum she'elah be'emet 'ishit vezeh hakol hergish kmo hatsagah vezeh pashut hayah me'atsben vemetaskel. lo' hitḥayvah leklum vebasuf zeh haya bizbuz zman.

I used to travel a lot to synagogues and Hebrew schools to recruit young campers and funds. One time in one school they gave me such [an exaggerated] welcome that it made me uncomfortable. The woman who met me was nice and polite in a way that felt fake and unpleasant; she was excited about whatever I said even though I knew her school had not previously cooperated with my organization. She showed interest in me without asking any real personal questions and everything felt like a performance, it was just annoying and frustrating. She never committed to anything, and it ended up being a waste of my time.

In Example 14, the Hebrew speaker was expecting a straightforward interaction; she was well aware of the instrumental context of this interaction, which made the positive social actions taken by her host (an "exaggerated" welcome, showing interest) come across as "fake." The actions did not achieve their goal of pleasing the addressee, who felt annoyed and frustrated. Once again, the American speaker's attempt to be "polite" was seen as "a waste of time," that is, completely unnecessary as well as inappropriate.

These examples illustrate the specific American English–Israeli Hebrew dyad. The Hebrew speakers evaluated the positive social acts deployed by the American English speakers as negatively exceeding expectations and therefore as over-polite. A speech community that deploys more politeness strategies than others, like the American one, is expectedly considered over-polite by speech communities that expect an absence of politeness strategies, like the Israeli one. However, this does not mean that Israelis cannot be "accused" of being over-polite by members of other cultures, even though their politeness norms entail directness and naturalness of speech. I asked a young American woman who had married an Israeli man and had been living in Israel for twelve years if she can recall any instance where Israelis were being too polite. She said:

15. If you consider being forcefully polite (Israelis trying to be friendly), then yes. Often, I would get asked super personal questions too fast (by a taxi driver or by colleagues in the workplace) in an attempt to establish a relationship, but timing was too fast.

In Example 15, the Anglo-American speaker is expecting nonpersonal questions in the context of the social distance between the interactants, while the Hebrew speaker in Example 14 expects just the opposite, namely "personal" questions that show the new acquaintance's interest in her. Thus, Examples 14 and 15 show different cultural expectations regarding the timing and nature of questions that serve to build a new relationship in specific situations. Both sides consider the performance of sociability a failure due to different social norms. The Anglo-American provided another illustrative example:

16. I would be at [my husband's] family for Shabbat dinner [and] they would want me to eat so badly, putting more and more food on my plate as if it were some sort of nicety to be putting food on my plate, but I couldn't eat all that it was sort of ridiculous.

Norms of hospitality and offerings of food manifest, inter alia, through linguistic politeness (Grainger et al., 2015). Knowing when, how, and how much food to offer is in cultural variation. These illustrative examples may indicate further differences in how Hebrew and American English speakers perceive sociability. The Anglo-American speaker's understanding of the Israeli norms of politeness and friendliness was that they were "forcefully friendly," which she considered too intimate ("super personal questions") for the context, or too hospitable (offering more and more food). These positive social acts that serve to build a relationship (getting to know one another) or demonstrate care (offering food) are perceived as inappropriate within the context and excessive, respectively.

Lastly, the Anglo-American added that she was accused of being too polite "all the time, for apologizing for something I didn't do, for being accommodating in circumstances that I should not accept, for saying I liked someone or something (like a party) when I didn't really mean it and being called out for it." Calling her out on her supposed overuse of positive social acts or insincere positive evaluation is in a way a face-threatening social action performed by Hebrew speakers. Intercultural settings in which speakers act according to what they know to be polite and appropriate but which fails as such in the new setting through no fault of their own can be experienced as frustrating and irritating and eventually lead to bad feelings toward the other culture. Intercultural contexts are prone to such misunderstandings and may, unfortunately, lead to stereotyping and national reputations (Spencer-Oatey & Kádár, 2021).

4.3.3 Strategic Use of Positive Social Actions

The third reason for positive social acts to be judged as over-polite is a detection of instrumentality – in other words, a perceived abuse or exploitation of positive social acts for personal benefit. Participants in an interaction can harness conventional positive social acts because of the expected positive effect (feeling good) from these acts. A detection of strategic intention may lead to a metapragmatic label of socially unacceptable use of language, such as flattery (Danziger, 2020). But if communication is always strategic (Goffman, 1967, 1970), it begs the question of why and how participants in an interaction judge the use of positive social acts as acceptable or unacceptable. Thus, for example, approbation aimed at "encouraging desired behavior" (Wolfson, 1984: 240) or oiling social relationships (Manes, 1983) is considered a positively marked compliment, but it entails the risk of being labeled flattery when it exceeds textual or contextual expectations (Holmes, 1986; Danziger, 2020).

Analyzing positive social acts that are labeled "flattery" is a helpful example because of flattery's ubiquity and reputation as a powerful tool to promote self-interest in popular and political literature, as well as in everyday conceptions. This is represented in English-language sayings like "flattery will get you everywhere (or nowhere)" and "imitation is the sincerest form of flattery." The power of flattery is represented in canonical writings, from Aesop's fable of "The Fox and the Crow," where the sly fox manipulates the crow to open its beak and part the cheese from its mouth, to Machiavelli's *The Prince* where lowly sycophants climb up the political ladder and gain power by strategically deploying positive social acts toward political actors. In these seminal works, discussions of flattery are usually accompanied by a warning against taking its sweet poison. Foucault ([1983] 2019) even goes so far as to see flattery as corrupt speech that stands in complete opposition to the moral truth of society. Plutarch ([ca. AD 110–120] 1927) offers a way to "tell a flatterer from a friend," demonstrating the challenge in distinguishing between manipulative and non-manipulative use of positive semiotic resources, especially when the poison is so sweet.

The power of flattery is derived from its strategic use of positive semiotic resources, that is, language that has the potential of creating a pleasing effect for the addressee. Creating that pleasing effect serves the flatterer because of two norms of reciprocity: reciprocal attraction and reciprocation of favor. Reciprocal attraction following flattery is created because "people find it hard not to like those who [appear to] think highly of them" (Jones, 1964: 24), and reciprocation of favor is achieved because people feel compelled to return a favor when one is given to them. The perception of flattery as being so powerful explains why despite it being socially unacceptable, it has continued to maintain its ubiquity throughout history to the present day across cultures and contexts. Social actors deploy flattery because of the plain fact that *it works* (Vonk, 2002).

Hypocrisy is another ubiquitous metapragmatic label for positive social acts used manipulatively. This moral behavior is judged as socially unacceptable when there is a perceived mismatch that is not intended to be detected between people's insincere claims and their actual deeds (Sorlin & Virtanen, 2021).

The American philosopher McKinnon (1991) claims that hypocrites are motivated by image management or, in pragmatic terms, the desire to present a better impression of their face. Impression management is acceptable social behavior (Goffman, 1967), but it crosses into unacceptable social behavior when the moral behavior is perceived as motivated and insincere impression management. Thus, similarly to flattery (crossing from acceptable strategic language like praise into unacceptable social behavior), hypocrisy is part of the "dark side" of social behavior. When moral behavior is interpreted as having strategic or instrumental intention, it is given a metapragmatic label of socially unacceptable use of positive social actions.

Though flattery and hypocrisy are examples of the "darker" side of sociability, or the strategic or manipulative abuse of positive social acts for the benefit of the speakers, they are not exceptions to language abuse. Language is always at risk of being used maliciously. Speakers and hearers are aware that language can be harnessed toward illegitimate ends, ranging from everyday manipulation (Sorlin, 2017) and deception (Galasinski, 2000) to the politically dangerous use of language, such as incitement (Kurzon, 1998) and propaganda (Steuter & Wills, 2010). While the perils of negative language use are quite obvious, the perils of exploiting positive social acts are not as clear, even though they are just as ubiquitous. For example, linguistic behavior that is intended to promote romantic or sexual relations can easily be experienced as "creepy" at best or as outright harassment at its worst. In the corpus collected for Section 3, an excerpt from a criminal law firm called Noga Wiesel described *firgun* from a male boss to a female employee as potential sexual harassment:

17. לאחרונה את מרגישה שיחסי העבודה הקורקטיים והמשימתיים שנרקמו בינך לבין המעביד שלך התחילו לקבל אופי שונה, ומעסיקך מרגיש איך לומר, פתוח יותר ואולי אף פתוח מדי לפרגן לך על מראך החיצוני ואף להעיר לך הערות סקסיסטיות או גסות? זוהי סיטואציה מביכה ומאיימת ללא ספק. את מרגישה בוודאי לא נוח עם המצב החדש שנוצר.

la'aḥronah 'at margishah sheyaḥasey ha'avodah hakorektiyim vehameś imatiym shenirkemu beynekh leben hama'avid shelakh hetḥilu lekabel 'ofi shoneh, vema'asikekh margish 'ekh lomer, patuaḥ miday lefargen lakh 'al mar'ekh haḥitsoni ve'af leha'ir lakh he'arot seksistiyot 'o gasot? Zohi situatsiya mevikhah veme'ayemet lelo' safek. 'at margishah bevad'ay lo' noaḥ 'im hamatsav haḥadash shenotsar.

Lately you have been feeling that the correct and task-oriented work relations between you and your employer have changed and your employer feels, let's say, more willing and even too willing to compliment [lit. *le-fargen;* INF] you about your appearance and even say sexist or lewd comments to you. This is an undoubtfully awkward and threatening situation. You must feel uncomfortable with the new circumstances.

In Example 17, the law firm describes instances where supposed "friendly" behavior in unequal work relations creates negative feelings and harm to the employee. The "positive" behavior (compliments on appearance) is inappropriate in this context (and of course in much wider contexts in life in general). This is an additional illustration of how intention is less important than accountability: It matters less how the boss intended his words or actions to be perceived or what the effect he was aiming for; if these actions were experienced as harmful, offensive, or threatening, he can be held accountable.

Instances like this – where there is a gap between the speaker's action and the hearer's interpretation – are fertile grounds for a discursive negotiation about meaning. Meanings can be negotiated on an interpersonal level, such as the workplace context of Example 17, but also on a public level, like in the "uncovered meat" incident described in Haugh (2008a) and in Section 4.1. Public political discourse follows slightly different norms than interpersonal discourse (Blum-Kulka & Weizman, 2003). The confrontational character of political discourse coupled with the prevalence of media in public life intensifies power struggles and the presence of conflicts and creates its own distinctive logic (Wodak, 2009; Kampf, 2013). Public scandals are often the source of public debate concerning intention, accountability, and the moral order, as many of the examples in this Element have shown (see also Thompson, 2000). A public context thus intensifies conflicts regarding the meaning and interpretation of positive communication and whether it will be perceived as positive or negative.

In political discourse, the manipulative use of positive social actions is also harmful on a wider scale. In a paper about political flattery, I outlined how, in democracies, the ritualization of public approbation by subordinates towards the leader are in fact cults of personality that have a detrimental effect on democratic processes (Danziger, 2021). In that paper, I showed that since political discourse is always considered strategic (Wilson, 2002), the line between acceptable and unacceptable use of positive language is not crossed when there is a perceived instrumental use of positive language, as in everyday discourse (Danziger, 2020). Instead, it is crossed when the use of approbation toward the leader is *ritualized*, conferring emblematic status on the political actor at the expense of the public. Habitually addressing public positive social actions that glorify the leader and approve their actions can lead to overconfidence and a consequent bias in decision-making. A leader who surrounds themselves with sycophants is not held accountable for their actions. Ritualized flattery thus harms the core democratic processes of accountability and decision-making. In the next section, I will illustrate the peril of using positive social actions through an example from an especially delicate context of public, political, and intercultural discourse.

4.4 The Peril of Over-Politeness: Flattery in Political Discourse in Intercultural Contexts

Judgment of positive social acts as unacceptable can stem from an evaluation of insincerity, ulterior motives, power relations, prejudice, a mismatch in pragmatic patterns, exaggerated or hyperbolic language, and a public context. I will illustrate this argument with an example from unused data I collected for a paper on flattery in cross-cultural contexts (Danziger & Kampf, 2021). In this paper, we did not analyze examples of political flattery, because political discourse follows slightly different norms. Searching for flattery items in a large online news website dataset from Sketch Engine in both Hebrew and Palestinian Arabic web corpora, we gathered 561 items in Hebrew (ḥanupaחנופה) and 43 in Palestinian Arabic (tamalluq تملق). Within that corpus, we encountered an unfortunate example of how positive social acts can fail miserably in an intercultural, public, political context: the intractable Israeli-Palestinian conflict.

The items in the realm of political discourse demonstrated three types of flattery. The first is using positive social acts as solidarity-enhancing tools to establish, promote, and restore relationships, which are inherent to the political game (Thompson, 2000). They are labeled flattery because political discourse is always considered strategic (Wilson, 2002). For example, in 2002, the chair of the Israeli Labor Party (Benjamin Ben Eliezer) prefaced an apology with a compliment as well as an expression of affection, saying, "I love you, Dalia. You are an excellent minister. I apologize for what I said that hurt you at the party convention." The strategic choice of a positive social act potentially increases the chances that his gesture would appease Dalia Itzik, the offended party member (Kampf & Danziger, 2019).

The second type is critical framing of a politician's positive social action by journalists as negative. If flattery is an evaluative label that implies an ascription of strategic or manipulative intent in the use of positive social acts, then a journalist who uses the label "flattery" to describe such an act by a political actor is not taking the positive social acts at face value. Explicit ascriptions of intentions are used not only to clarify but also to criticize a social action (Deppermann & Haugh, 2022). By giving these actions a label of unaccepted positive behavior, journalists are implicitly criticizing their use in a specific context. For example, a news article was published on Haaretz.co.il in 2018 under the headline "The ritual of kissing Netanyahu's ass has gone too far: Jackie Levi outdoes Ayub Kara."[23] In this article, the journalist Rogel Alper

---

[23] "The ritual of kissing Netanyahu's ass has gone too far: Jackie Levi outdoes Ayub Kara," Haaretz.co.il website, October 11, 2018 (www.haaretz.co.il/gallery/television/tv-review/ 1.6548143?utm_source=App_Share&utm_medium=iOS_Native) (accessed March 8, 2022).

accused the Likud member Jackie Levi of flattering the then prime minister Benjamin Netanyahu by displaying appreciation and admiration of Netanyahu's wife, Sarah, when the prime minister attended Levi's rally. By using the label of flattery, journalists fulfill their professional goal of criticizing political action they see as harmful to the public. In this case, the ritualistic flattery toward Netanyahu (Danziger, 2021).

The third type is accusations of flattery by rival actors. Like journalists, political actors can publicly frame positive social acts used by their rivals as flattery in order to express criticism regarding their strategic or manipulative use. For example, in 2016 MK Michal Rozin, a member of the opposition, accused the then prime minister Netanyahu and the "right wing government" of publicly flattering the settlers by promoting tourism to Bet-El, a Jewish settlement over the Green Line.[24] By labeling the actions that benefited one group over the other as flattery, Rozin criticized the government's actions. By publicly using the label of flattery, political actors can harm the reputation of their rivals as well as strengthen their own electoral base.

The analyzed corpus contained recurrent accusations of flattery from both sides toward political actors in the conflict when an action was perceived as being favorable to the "enemy." That is, when an Israeli political figure used positive social actions toward Palestinians, his actions received a negative judgment by the Israeli public and the same goes for Palestinian political figures who use positive social actions toward Israelis (see also Kampf & David [2019], who used experimental methods to reach this conclusion in relation to the Israeli public). In the following example from the Israeli news platform Rotter.net,[25] a Hebrew speaker accuses the late prime minister Yitzhak Rabin of a flattering speech toward an undeserving recipient. The speech in question was given by Rabin on July 26, 1994, to the US Congress in Washington. The previous day, Israel and Jordan had signed the Washington Declaration, in which both states announced the end of the "state of belligerency" and expressed a joint ambition to reach a peace treaty between them. A formal peace treaty was subsequently signed later that year, on October 26, 1994. Rabin's speech was about his wish to end war and promote a peace process. Rabin's conciliatory policy toward Israel's Arab neighbors, and especially his support of the Oslo Accords, was heavily criticized by many Israelis at the time, who considered his actions

---

[24] "MK Rozin on the Bet-El project: The government is flattering settlers," Walla! Website, October 6, 2016 (https://news.walla.co.il/item/3003505) (accessed March 8, 2022). The Green Line was Israel's border until the 1967 war. Building Jewish settlements over the Green Line is politically controversial.

[25] See the Rotter.net website at https://rotter.net/forum/gil/5515.shtml (accessed August 5, 2022).

appeasing to an aggressive enemy who does not want real peace. Approximately one year later, on November 4, 1995, Rabin was assassinated by a man who objected to his policy. The post in Example 18 was written in 2004 on Rotter.net, a web platform that allows for forum discussions. The post was written in a discussion thread responding to Rabin's peace speeches that were published in a book in 1995.[26]

18. הנאום גדוש לעייפה דברי חנופה לאויב הערבי. בנאומו מצייר רבין את הערבים כעם שחלום
חייו הוא השלום והשקט, בעוד שמאה השנים האחרונות הוכיחו את ההיפך הגמור (...) יש
בנאום הזה מליצות, שרק רכיכות חסרי חוליות מסוגלים להוציא מקולמוסם: למשל, המליצה
על "צחוקו של התינוק בעמן שמעיר ישנים בירושלים העברית", או המליצה על כך ש"שני
העמים יושבים בצילה של אותה תאנה ואוכלים מפריו של אותו גפן" – אלה הן מליצות רוויות
חנופה חולנית, שמבטאות פחד ממלחמה – פחד שגורר מתן מחמאות ללא כיסוי לאויב צמא
דמים, פחד שגורר היסמכות על אשליות בדבר אנושיותו של האויב.

han'um gadush le'aifah divrey ḥanupa la'oyev ha'aravi. bene'umo metsayer rabin 'et ha'aravim ke'am sheḥalom ḥayav hu' hashalom vehashket, be'od sheme'ah hashanim ha'aḥronot hokhiḥu 'et hahefekh gagamur (...) yesh bane'um hazeh melitsot, sherak rekikhot ḥasrey ḥuliyot mesugalim lehotsi' mikulmusam: lemashal, hamelitsah 'al "tsḥoko shel hatinok be'aman she-me'ir yeshenim beyerushalayim ha'ivrit", 'o hamelitsah 'al kakh sh"shney ha'amim yoshvim betsilah shel 'otah te'enah ve'okhlim meperav shel 'oto gefen" – 'eleh hen melitsot revuyot ḥanupa ḥolanit, shemevat'ot paḥad memilḥamah – paḥad shegorer matan maḥma'ot lelo' kisuy le'oyev tsme damim, paḥad shegorer hisamkhut 'al 'ashlayot bedvar 'enushiyuto she ha'oyev.

The speech was overflowing with flattery of the Arab enemy. In his speech, Rabin paints the Arabs as a people striving for peace and quiet, while the past one hundred years have proved the exact opposite (. . .) this speech is full of superfluous tropes that only spineless shellfish [a common saying in Hebrew] can extract from their pen: for example, the trope about the "baby's laughter in Amman that can wake the sleeping in [the Hebrew part of] Jerusalem," or the one about "two peoples sitting under the same fig tree and eating from the same grape vine" – these are tropes brimming with sickening flattery that indicate a fear of war – a fear that leads to empty compliments [extended to] a bloodthirsty enemy [and] a delusional reliance on the humanity of the enemy.

Rabin's conciliatory speech is negatively labeled by the writer of the post as "sickening" flattery. The Hebrew speaker's rhetoric demonstrates a perception of "the Arab" as an enemy and undeserving of a solidarity-enhancing action.

---

[26] Though not published in English, the book's title can be approximately translated as "Peace Chaser: The Peace Speeches of Prime Minister Yitzhak Rabin." The book is published by Zmora Bitan (in Hebrew).

He interprets Rabin's tropes about the coexistence of Jews and Arabs as superfluous, weak, and unrightfully trying to appease a bloodthirsty enemy. Appeasing is "the action of satisfying the demands of an aggressive person, country, or organization."[27] Flattery and appeasement overlap in that they are positive social acts that are negatively evaluated in political discourse. Appeasement has extremely negative connotations in political history, following the response of the UK in the 1930s to German military attempts to take more land (Goddard, 2015). Political actors who speak favorably toward the enemy and therefore practice appeasement are deemed "spineless shellfish" by the writer of the post, leaders who "fear war" and give out "empty compliments" and who will be exploited and overtaken by the enemy. Positive action and communication in this political conflict are perceived as weak, foolish, and even dangerous.

Example 19 is from alhourriah.ps, a Palestinian news magazine called Freedom.[28] The magazine is affiliated with the socialist Democratic Front for the Liberation of Palestine (DFLP). The DFLP opposes serving in governments under the Palestinian Authority and has been critical of their policies, particularly regarding security coordination with Israel.[29] The text is from an article published in 2007. At the time, Hamas had recently seized the Gaza Strip. Diab Al-Ali, the commander of the Palestinian National Security Forces, had been coordinating with Israeli security forces. The writer of the article accuses him of flattering the "enemy" by communicating with the Israeli security forces:

19. القادة الذين لا يخجلون من التنسيق الامني مع الاعداء هؤلاء هم الذين يعيبون على شعبهم المقاومة و يفتخرون بالتنسيق الامني مع المحتلين. ان تصريحات ذياب العلي معيبة و ضارة و مسيئة لشعب فلسطين, (...) تصريحات العلي تعبر عن عجز و ضيق افق و ارتماء في احضان اعداء الشعب الفلسطيني و تملق للمحتلين و مزايدة رخيصة على الاخرين في فتح و السلطة قبل غيرهم.

al-qādah al-ladhīna lā yakhjalūna min al-tansīq al-amnī ma'a al-a'dā' ha'ulā' hum al-ladhīna ya'ībūna 'alá sha'bihim al-muqāwamah wa-yaftakhirūna bi-l-tansīq al-amnī ma'a al-muḥtallīn. inna taṣrīḥāt Dhiyāb al-'Alī ma'ībah wa-ḍārrah wa-musī'ah li-sha'b filasṭīn (…) taṣrīḥāt al-'Alī tu'abbiru 'an 'ajz wa-ḍayq ufuq wa-irtimā' fī aḥḍān a'dā' al-sha'b al-filasṭīnī wa-tamalluq lil-muḥtallīn wa-muzāyadah rakhīṣah 'alá al-ākharīn fī fatḥ wa-al-sulṭah qabla ghayrihim.

---

[27] See the definition of "appeasing," in *Cambridge Dictionary*, Cambridge Dictionaries Online website (https://dictionary.cambridge.org/dictionary/english/appease) (accessed February 24, 2022).

[28] I thank Jonathan Mey-Tal for transcribing the text according to the Library of Congress Romanization norms and Raida Aiashe-Khatib for translating the text to English.

[29] See "Democratic Change (DFLP)," Mapping Palestinian Politics website (https://ecfr.eu/special/mapping_palestinian_politics/democratic-change) (accessed August 23, 2022).

> Leaders who are not ashamed of security coordination with their enemies
> are those who criticize their own people's resistance and take pride in
> security coordination with the occupiers. The declarations of Diab Al-Ali
> are defective, harmful, and offensive to the people of Palestine (. . .)
> Al-Ali's statements express impotence, narrowness of sight, and throwing
> themselves into the arms of the enemies of the Palestinian people, flatter-
> ing the occupiers, and a cheap bidding for others in Fatah and the author-
> ity in the first hand.

The writer of the post considers the Israeli side an enemy, calling the Israeli forces "the occupiers." Any coordination between Palestinian and Israeli security forces is considered an acknowledgment of Israel's authority and therefore cooperation with the Israeli "occupiers." Cooperation between Israeli and Palestinian security forces entails communication between the authorities and the sharing of intelligence in order to prevent acts of terror. Any communication with "the enemy" is marked because no communication is the expected action (or nonaction). In this example, communication and cooperation with Israel were evaluated negatively as "defective, harmful and offensive." The Arabic speaker perceives the positive action of coordination through communication with the other side as appeasing flattery that will eventually lead to their downfall. Like the Hebrew speaker, he too considers people who are using positive communication toward an undeserving enemy as weak, saying "Al-Ali's statements express impotence." Examples 18 and 19 demonstrate that both sides of the conflict accuse their leaders of dangerous flattery when they act favorably toward the other side, undermining the potential of flattery to create solidarity and rapport (Danziger, 2020).

These examples indicate that each side considers the other an enemy who is underserving of positive communication, or even just communication. Rabin's conciliatory speech was meant to "extend a hand in peace," but it did not achieve its pacifying end (Gavriely-Nuri, 2010), and the commander of the Palestinian National Security Forces Diab Al-Ali was trying to prevent terror by communicating with the Israeli forces. In this disadvantageous context of the Israeli-Palestinian intractable conflict, the "other" always seems to be underserving of positive communication, which leads to mutual accusations of flattery. If the outgroup is always underserving, when do political positive social actions achieve their pacifying ends in an interstate context? Two recent studies, Kampf et al. (2021) and Chudi and Kampf (2022), have tried to tackle this difficult question. These studies analyze online responses to amicable public messages by leaders perceived, from the Israeli perspective, as "controversial" in the context of the Israeli-Palestinian conflict. Their findings indicate that amicable messages from a Palestinian leader are negatively evaluated more frequently than messages from non-Palestinian leaders (Western and Middle Eastern). They conclude that the identity of the Palestinian leader has a negative association due to frequent negative encounters and experiences with Palestinian representatives and their constant presence in the Israeli news. Therefore, if an amicable message is delivered by a Western or Middle Eastern leader, it has better chances of achieving its conciliatory end. It is therefore the identity of the speaker that determines if a positive social act will be perceived as positive or negative in the context of the Israel-Palestinian conflict. In the Conclusion, I will attempt to provide an answer for the parallel question that has driven this Element (pertaining to nonpolitical contexts), that is, when are positive social actions evaluated positively and when do they become negative over-politeness?

4.5 Summary

In this section, I have discussed negatively marked positive social action, that is, positive communication that is evaluated negatively as exceeding appropriateness. First, I have outlined the elements of over-politeness by exploring the semantic field of over-friendly behaviors that have a metapragmatic label in English, such as fawning, toadying, ingratiating, and so on. What all these friendly behaviors have in common is that speakers somewhat exploit, for their own benefit, the positive effect expected from these positive social actions. Because they have a conventional label in language, I concluded that they are socially coded norm violations: behaviors that are known to exceed acceptability of positive social actions use.

Followingly, I described the contexts of over-politeness and offered illustrative examples for each: failed politeness (or relational mismanagement), intercultural pragmatic failures, and strategic use of positive communication. The examples in this section have shown that positive social actions that are evaluated as over-polite can receive a metapragmatic label such as "creepy" or metapragmatic comments like "aggressively friendly," but their evaluation can also be detected through uptake (as in Izadi, 2016). They have also demonstrated that over-politeness is mostly taken negatively, with a few exceptions, such as failed politeness in a close relationship or harmless flattery. And lastly, they have demonstrated the role of social norms and expectations regarding the appropriate use of positive social actions within a specific culture.

The three contexts in which we are likely to find evaluations of over-politeness demonstrate that over-politeness is unintended: either the speaker unknowingly applies pragmatic patterns incorrectly (intra-culturally or inter-culturally) or uses strategic positive language that is meant to be positively marked (in this case, the speaker takes a calculated risk in their instrumental use of positive language). The over-polite label is a product of the nonspeaker participant's judgment of the utterance as such.[30] Although over-politeness is unintentional, addressees or observers nonetheless evaluate what the speaker intended by their utterance. A judgment of a positive social act as unacceptable can stem from an evaluation of insincerity, ulterior motives, power relations, prejudice, a mismatch in pragmatic patterns, exaggerated or hyperbolic language, a public context, and other possible reasons. The examples from the Israeli-Palestinian conflict in Section 4.4 demonstrate that, in some contexts, such as in an interactable conflict, positive social actions are even more likely to fail and cause further relational harm.

5 Conclusion

This Element has defined positive social actions as social behaviors that are aimed to establish, promote, or restore relationships. They include conventional speech acts such as compliments, praise, thanks, congratulations and good wishes, rapport-enhancement strategies like seeking common ground, sharing a laugh, and showing support. Generally speaking, this includes any positive communication that is aimed at making the other feel good and promote sociability. These social acts are the building blocks of positive communication because of their expected effect on sociability. In order for positive communication to achieve its goal of advancing sociability, it must be perceived as positive. This is the point of contact between positive and polite communication: Positive social acts are relational work that is evaluated in context. Positive and polite communication are sometimes used interchangeably, but positive social actions are not always appropriate, polite, or evaluated positively; sometimes they are inappropriate, impolite, or evaluated negatively. The evaluation of positive social actions as polite communication depends on what interactants expect in terms of text, context, and sociocultural norms.

In order to discuss the "bright" side of sociability, that is, positively marked positive social actions, and the "dark" side of sociability, that is, negatively marked positive social actions, this Element drew on a metapragmatic methodology. Metapragmatic labels and comments ensured a discussion of positive and negative evaluations from the interactants' point of view. Additionally,

---

[30] Similarly, Culpeper (2011) notes that impoliteness does not have to be intended; people can be hurt, insulted, or offended by meanings even when speakers did not intend to offend (although it certainly can be intended).

metapragmatic comments often revealed the interpretation process that inter-actants went through before concluding if the positive social actions were appropriate or inappropriate, politic or non-politic, or even impolite. In Section 3, the metapragmatic label of *firgun* was used to collect and analyze positively marked positive social actions in the Hebrew-speaking community. The analysis showed the gamut of positive social actions that fall under the emic term for positive communication and revealed the pragmatic moral order of Hebrew speakers as being based on sincere support and reciprocity. Thus, in that section, we saw how positive communication promotes sociability and in what cases it meets or positively exceeds expectations.

In Section 4, I went on to discuss negatively marked positive social actions, that is, over-politeness. After exploring the semantic field of over-polite and over-friendly behaviors that have a metapragmatic label in English, I outlined the three contexts in which we can encounter over-politeness: failed politeness (or relational mismanagement), intercultural pragmatic failures, and strategic use of positive communication. Through examples from the Israeli-Palestinian conflict, we saw how, in some contexts, positive social actions are more likely to fail than succeed, and even cause further relational harm.

This Element has shown the benefits and perils of deploying positive social acts in interaction. Positive social actions are a powerful relational tool; they can greatly advance sociability, but they can also derail it. A compliment can promote solidarity in first encounters between people, but it can also cause public scandal or be perceived as sexual harassment. The same exact action can be interpreted as positive or negative in different contexts (e.g., intimate relationships vs. complete strangers). As we have seen in Section 4, a personal question from someone you just met can be seen as expected and positive by a Hebrew speaker but as unexpected and negative by an Anglo-American. Even the same action in the same context can be interpreted as positive or negative by different people because of different roles in a situational context. The receiver of a positive evaluation can see it as a compliment, while an observer can judge the action as flattery. Therefore, there is a fuzzy line between appropriate and inappropriate posi-tive communication and between acceptable and unacceptable positive behavior.

The success or failure of positive communication is not clear-cut. Some examples described in this Element, especially those in public contexts, have pointed out the potential gap between the speaker's actions and the hearer's (or observer's) interpretation. Although interactants do not have access to the actual intentions of the speaker, they nonetheless evaluate these intentions, by noting text and context. Intention is often debated, both in interpersonal (e.g., interactional misunderstandings) and in public contexts (e.g., a public debate following a scandal). The ambiguity of intention and the evaluative nature of politeness support the distinction between positive and polite communication. By distinguishing between action and attitude, we can see how no action is inherently positive; it requires meeting expectations regarding text, context, and the moral order of a specific culture.

Each linguaculture will have a specific relational work continuum wherein, at one point, use of positive language crosses into unacceptable. The social action of labeling certain behaviors as appropriate at times and inappropriate at others stems from the pragmatic knowledge of a specific speech community. Judging a compliment as inappropriate or impolite entails a knowledge of what is an appropriate compliment. The existence of common or conventional metaprag-matic labels like "back-handed compliment" and "empty compliment" suggests that it is not always easy to decipher what speakers do with words. The evaluation of a positive social action as inappropriate varies across time and culture, and there is also individual variation (that can change with time, too). Cultures change, languages change, and people change.

The discussion in this Element leads to the age-old conclusion that human experience is fuzzy and dynamic. Sociability is not neatly organized into categories, of positive and negative. Categorization is a human activity, an attempt to grasp a complex existence (Geertz, 1973). Alas, we continue to try and categorize social interaction, like positive and negative, positive and polite, polite and impolite. We do that because categorization creates clarity and order. So, after doing just that in this Element, this Conclusion celebrates the fuzziness of social relations, as a dynamic and relative experience.

A Möbius strip can serve as a visual metaphor for sociability.[31] Borrowed from mathematics, by all accounts a precise science, a Möbius strip is a non-orientable surface, in which consistent orientation is meaningless, that is, no north or south, no right or left, no negative or positive poles. A Möbius strip can be created by taking a paper strip and giving it a half-twist, and then joining the ends of the strip together to form a loop (see Figure 3).[32]

The Möbius strip has two seemingly separate poles that, in reality, function as the inverse and obverse of the same structural surface. The only way to grasp their relation is through constantly shifting our perspective between the two points. This visual metaphor embraces the fuzziness of social interaction by representing the bright and dark sides of sociability not as opposed to one

---

[31] The credit for this idea goes to Tamar Katriel, who suggested it to me after attending a presentation on flattery that I gave to the Israeli Discourse Group at the Hebrew University in 2021. I wish to thank her very much for this wonderful suggestion.

[32] I thank Maayan Karlinski-Zur for creating this figure.

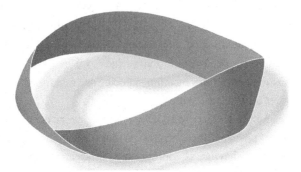

Figure 3 The Möbius strip as a visual metaphor for sociability.

another but as created alongside one another on a non-orientable surface or plane. In the same way that we cannot define relative concepts on their own, that is, good without bad or positive without negative, conceptualizing sociability as a Möbius strip suggests that perhaps creating a dichotomy of brighter and darker sides is insufficient for pragmatic analysis. Categorizing form and function, a common pragmatic practice, only provides a partial understanding of social phenomena like positive (and negative) communication. The Möbius strip aids in understanding that social actions, and, within them, positive social acts and their evaluation in context, are relative constructs; what person A considers polite can be considered impolite by person B at the exact same time. The Möbius strip helps visualize this complexity in that pinning linguistic behaviors on it is theoretically impossible. Placing linguistic behaviors on a continuum may help the academic endeavor to classify the evaluation of a certain uptake (as positive or negative, appropriate or inappropriate, etc.), but sociability and language use are in fact more fluid than that. It is more productive to visualize the bright and dark sides of sociability as inseparable, intertwined, and possibly defining one another. Shifting between the two is a matter of perspective.

References

Abadi, A. (1991). Speech acts of public apologies. In M. Goshen, S. Morag, & S. Kogot, eds., *Shai Le-Chaim Rabin*. Jerusalem: Academon [in Hebrew], pp. 257–72.

Arundale, R. B. (2006). Face as relational and interactional: A communication framework for research on face, facework, and politeness. *Journal of Politeness Research*, **2**(2), 193–216. https://doi.org/10.1515/PR.2006.011.

Arundale, R. B. (2013). Face as a research focus in interpersonal pragmatics: Relational and emic perspectives. *Journal of Pragmatics*, **58**, 108–120.

Barnlund, D. C. & Araki, S. (1985). Intercultural encounters: The management of compliments by Japanese and Americans. *Journal of Cross-Cultural Psychology*, **16**(1), 9–26.

Beale, W. H. (1978). Rhetorical performative discourse: A new theory of epideictic. *Philosophy & Rhetoric*, **11**(4): 221–46. www.jstor.org/stable/40237084.

Blum-Kulka, S. (1990). You don't touch lettuce with your fingers: Parental politeness in family discourse. *Journal of Pragmatics*, **14**(2), 259–88. https://doi.org/10.1016/0378-2166(90)90083-P.

Blum-Kulka, S. ([1992] 2005). The meta-pragmatics of politeness in Israeli society. In R. Watts, S. Ide, & K. Ehlich, eds., *Politeness in Language*. 2nd ed. Berlin: Mouton de Gruyter, pp. 255–80. https://doi.org/10.1515/9783110886542.

Blum-Kulka, S., House, J., & Kasper, G. (1989). *Cross-Cultural Pragmatics: Requests and Apologies*. Advances in Discourse Processes, Vol. 31. Norwood, NJ: Ablex.

Blum-Kulka, S. & Katriel, T. (1991). Nicknaming practices in families: A cross-cultural perspective. In S. Ting-Toomey & F. Korzenny, eds., *Cross-Cultural Interpersonal Communication*. Newbury Park, CA: Sage Publications, pp. 58–78.

Blum-Kulka, S. & Olshtain, E. (1984). Requests and apologies: A cross-cultural study of speech act realization patterns (CCSARP). *Applied Linguistics*, **5**(3), 196–213. https://doi.org/10.1093/applin/5.3.196.

Blum-Kulka, S. & Weizman, E. (2003). Misunderstandings in political interviews. In J. House, G. Kasper, & S. Rosse, eds., *Misunderstanding in Social Life: Discourse Approaches to Problematic Talk*. New York: Routledge, pp. 104–25.

Brooks, D. J. & Geer, J. G. (2007). Beyond negativity: The effects of incivility on the electorate. *American Journal of Political Science*, **51**(1), 1–16.

Brown, G. & Yule, G. (1983). *Discourse Analysis*. Cambridge: Cambridge University Press.

Brown, P. & Levinson, S. (1987). *Politeness: Some Universals in Language Use*. Cambridge: Cambridge University Press.

Caffi, C. (1998). Metapragmatics. In J. Mey, ed., *The Concise Encyclopedia of Pragmatics*. Amsterdam: Elsevier, pp. 581–86.

Cameron, D. (2004). Out of the bottle: The social life of metalanguage. In A. Jaworski, N. Coupland, & D. Galasinski, eds., *Metalanguage: Social and Ideological Perspectives*. Berlin and New York: Mouton de Gruyter, pp. 311–21. https://doi.org/10.1515/9783110907377.

Chang, W. & Fukushima, S. (2017). "Your care and concern are my burden": Accounting for the emic concepts of "attentiveness" and "empathy" in interpersonal relationships among Taiwanese females. *East Asian Pragmatics*, **2**(1), 1–23. https://doi.org/10.1558/eap.33081.

Chudi, D. & Kampf, Z. (2022). It's the messenger: Identity-based evaluation of amicable messages during conflict. *The Journal of Public Opinion Research*, **34**(1), 1–21. https://doi.org/10.1093/ijpor/edac008.

Culpeper, J. (2008). Reflections on impoliteness, relational work and power. In D. Bousfield & M. A. Locher, eds., *Impoliteness in Language: Studies on Its Interplay with Power in Theory and Practice*. Language, Power and Social Processes, Vol. 21. Berlin: Mouton de Gruyter, pp. 17–44.

Culpeper, J. (2011). *Impoliteness: Using Language to Cause Offence*. Studies in Interactional Sociolinguistics, Vol. 28. Cambridge: Cambridge University Press.

Culpeper, J., O'Driscoll, J., & Hardaker, C. (2019). Notions of politeness in Britain and North America. In E. Ogiermann & P. Garcés-Conejos Blitvich, eds., *From Speech Acts to Lay Understandings of Politeness: Multilingual and Multicultural Perspectives*. Cambridge: Cambridge University Press, pp. 176–200.

Culpeper, J. & Tantucci, V. (2021). The principle of (im)politeness reciprocity. *Journal of Pragmatics*, **175**, 146–64. https://doi.org/10.1016/j.pragma.2021.01.008.

Danziger, R. (2018). Compliments and compliment responses in Israeli Hebrew: Hebrew university in Jerusalem students in interaction. *Journal of Pragmatics*, **124**, 73–87. https://doi.org/10.1016/j.pragma.2017.12.004.

Danziger, R. (2020). The pragmatics of flattery: The strategic use of solidarity-oriented actions. *Journal of Pragmatics*, **170**, 413–25. https://doi.org/10.1016/j.pragma.2020.09.027.

Danziger, R. (2021). The democratic king: Ritualized flattery in political discourse. *Discourse & Society*. **32**(6), 645–65. https://doi.org/10.1177/09579265211023224.

Danziger, R. & Kampf, Z. (2021). Interpretive constructs in contrast: The case of flattery in Hebrew and in Palestinian Arabic. *Contrastive Pragmatics*, 2(2), 137–67. https://doi.org/10.1163/26660393-BJA10020.

Deppermann, A. & Haugh, M. (eds.). (2022). *Action Ascription in Interaction*. Studies in Interactional Sociolinguistics, Vol. 35. Cambridge: Cambridge University Press.

Dori-Hacohen, G. (2016). *Tokbek* [Talk-back], Israeli speech economy, and other non-deliberative terms for political talk. In D. Carbaugh, ed., *The Handbook of Communication in Cross-Cultural Perspective*. New York and London: Routledge, pp. 299–311.

Du, P. (2022). Shared laughter as relational strategy at intercultural conflictual workplace interactions. *Journal of Pragmatics*, **188**, 39–55. https://doi.org/10.1016/j.pragma.2021.11.016.

Du Bois, J. W. (2007). The stance triangle. In R. Englebretson, ed., *Stancetaking in Discourse: Subjectivity, Evaluation, Interaction*. Amsterdam: John Benjamins, pp. 139–82.

Dumitrescu, D. (2006). Noroc!; Merci;! que lindo!; sorry: Some polite speech acts across cultures. *Southwest Journal of Linguistics*, **25**(2), 1–38.

Economidou-Kogetsidis, M. (2011). "Please answer me as soon as possible": Pragmatic failure in non-native speakers' e-mail requests to faculty. *Journal of Pragmatics*, **43**(13), 3193–215. https://doi.org/10.1016/j.pragma.2011.06.006.

Eelen, G. (2001). *A Critique of Politeness Theories*. Manchester: St. Jerome Publishing.

Eisenstein, M. & Bodman, J. (1993). Expressing gratitude in American English. In G. Kasper & S. Blum-Kulka, eds., *Interlanguage Pragmatics*. Oxford: Oxford University Press, pp. 64–81.

Faulkner, P. (2018). Giving the benefit of the doubt. *International Journal of Philosophical Studies*, **26**(2), 139–55. https://doi.org/10.1080/09672559.2018.1440952.

Fehr, E. & Fischbacher, U. (2004). Social norms and human cooperation. *Trends in Cognitive Sciences*, **8**(4), 185–90.

First, A. & Avraham, E. (2009). *America in Jerusalem: Globalization, National Identity, and Israeli Advertising*. Lanham, MD: Lexington Books.

Foucault, M. ([1983] 2019). *Discourse and Truth and Parresia*. Chicago, IL: University of Chicago Press.

Fukushima, S. (2009). Evaluation of politeness: Do the Japanese evaluate attentiveness more positively than the British? *Pragmatics*, **19**(4), 501–18.

Fukushima, S. (2019). A metapragmatic aspect of politeness: With a special emphasis on attentiveness in Japanese. In E. Ogiermann & P. Garcés-Conejos

Blitvich, eds., *From Speech Acts to Lay Understandings of Politeness: Multilingual and Multicultural Perspectives*. Cambridge: Cambridge University Press, pp. 226–47.

Galasinski, D. (2000). *The Language of Deception: A Discourse Analytical Study*. Thousand Oaks, CA: Sage Publications.

Gavriely-Nuri, D. (2010). If both opponents "extend hands in peace" – why don't they meet?: Mythic metaphors and cultural codes in the Israeli peace discourse. *Journal of Language and Politics*, **9**(3), 449–68.

Geertz, C. (1973). *The Interpretation of Cultures*. New York: Basic Books.

Goddard, S. E. (2015). The rhetoric of appeasement: Hitler's legitimation and British foreign policy, 1938–39. *Security Studies*, **24**(1), 95–130. https://doi.org/10.1080/09636412.2015.1001216.

Goffman, E. (1967). *Interaction Ritual: Essays on Face-to-Face Interaction*. 1st ed. Garden City, NY: Anchor Books.

Goffman, E. (1970). *Strategic Interaction*. Oxford: Blackwell.

Goodwin, C. (1994). Professional vision. *American Anthropologist*, **96**(3), 606–33. www.jstor.org/stable/682303.

Grainger, K., Kerkam, Z., Mansor, F., & Mills, S. (2015). Offering and hospitality in Arabic and English. *Journal of Politeness Research*, **11**(1), 41–70. https://doi.org/10.1515/pr-2015-0003.

Haugh, M. (2008a). Intention and diverging interpretings of implicature in the "uncovered meat" sermon. *Intercultural Pragmatics*, **5**(2), 201–28. https://doi.org/10.1515/IP.2008.011.

Haugh, M. (2008b). Intention in pragmatics. *Intercultural Pragmatics*, **5**(2), 99–110. https://doi.org/10.1515/IP.2008.006.

Haugh, M. (2010). Jocular mockery, (dis)affiliation, and face. *Journal of Pragmatics*, **42**(8), 2106–19. https://doi.org/10.1016/j.pragma.2009.12.018.

Haugh, M. (2013). Im/politeness, social practice and the participation order. *Journal of Pragmatics*, **58**, 52–72. https://doi.org/10.1016/j.pragma.2013.07.003.

Haugh, M. (2016). The role of English as a scientific metalanguage for research in pragmatics: Reflections on the metapragmatics of "politeness" in Japanese. *East Asian Pragmatics*, **1**(1), 41–73. https://doi.org/10.1558/eap.v1i1.27610.

Haugh, M. (2019). The metapragmatics of consideration in (Australian and New Zealand) English. In E. Ogiermann & P. Garcés-Conejos Blitvich, eds., *From Speech Acts to Lay Understandings of Politeness: Multilingual and Multicultural Perspectives*. Cambridge: Cambridge University Press, pp. 201–25.

Hauser, G. A. (1999). Aristotle on epideictic: The formation of public morality. *Rhetoric Society Quarterly*, **29**(1), 5–23.

Hay, J. (2001). The pragmatics of humor support. *Humor: International Journal of Humor Research*, **14**(1), 55–82. https://doi.org/10.1515/humr.14.1.55.

Holmes, J. (1986). Compliments and compliment responses in New Zealand English. *Anthropological Linguistics*, **28**(4), 485–508.

Holmes, J. & Marra, M. (2004). Relational practice in the workplace: Women's talk or gendered discourse? *Language in Society*, **33**(3), 377–398. https://doi.org/10.1017/S0047404504043039.

Ide, S., Hill, B., Carnes, Y., Ogino, T., & Kawasaki, A. (1992). The concept of politeness: An empirical study of American English and Japanese. In R. Watts, S. Ide, & K. Ehlich, eds., *Politeness in Language: Studies in Its History, Theory and Practice*. (pp. 281–297). Berlin: Mouton de Gruyter.

Isosävi, J. (2020). Cultural outsiders' reported adherence to Finnish and French politeness norms. *Journal of Pragmatics*, **155**, 177–92. https://doi.org/10.1016/j.pragma.2019.10.015.

Izadi, A. (2016). Over-politeness in Persian professional interactions. *Journal of Pragmatics*, **102**, 13–23. https://doi.org/10.1016/j.pragma.2016.06.004.

Jamieson, K. H., Volinsky, A., Weitz, I., & Kenski, K. (2017). The political uses and abuses of civility and incivility. In K. Kenski & K. Jamieson, eds., *The Oxford Handbook of Political Communication*. Oxford: Oxford University Press, pp. 205–18.

Jaworski, A. (1994). Pragmatic failure in a second language: Greeting responses in English by Polish students. *IRAL: International Review of Applied Linguistics in Language Teaching*, **32**(1), 41–56. https://doi.org/10.1515/iral.1994.32.1.41.

Jaworski, A. (1995). "This is not an empty compliment!": Polish compliments and the expression of solidarity. *International Journal of Applied Linguistics*, **5**(1), 63–94.

Jones, E. E. (1964). *Ingratiation: A Social Psychological Analysis*. New York: Appleton-Century-Crofts.

Jucker, A. H. & Taavitsainen. I. (2014). Complimenting in the history of American English: A metacommunicative expression analysis. In I. Taavitsainen, A. H. Jucker, & J. Tuominen, eds., *Diachronic Corpus Pragmatics*. Pragmatics and Beyond New Series 243. Amsterdam: John Benjamins, pp. 257–76.

Kádár, D. Z. & Haugh, M. (2013). *Understanding Politeness*. Cambridge: Cambridge University Press.

Kampf, Z. (2008). The pragmatics of forgiveness: Judgments of apologies in the Israeli political arena. *Discourse & Society*, **19**(5), 577–98. https://doi.org/10.1177/0957926508092244.

Kampf, Z. (2009). Public (non-) apologies: The discourse of minimizing responsibility. *Journal of Pragmatics*, **41**(11), 2257–70. https://doi.org/10.1016/j.pragma.2008.11.007.

Kampf, Z. (2013). Mediated performatives. In J. Verschueren & J. Östman, eds., *Handbook of Pragmatics*. Amsterdam: John Benjamins, pp. 1–24.

Kampf, Z. (2016). All the best! Performing solidarity in political discourse. *Journal of Pragmatics*, **93**, 47–60. https://doi.org/10.1016/j.pragma.2015.12.006.

Kampf, Z., Aldar, L., Danziger, R., & Schreiber, M. (2019). The pragmatics of amicable interstate communication. *Intercultural Pragmatics*, **16**(2), 123–51. https://doi.org/10.1515/ip-2019-0007.

Kampf, Z., Chudy, D., Danziger, R., & Schreiber, M. (2021). "Wait with falling in love": Discursive evaluation of amicable messages conveyed by opponents. *Journal of Language and Social Psychology*, **40**(2), 188–213. https://doi.org/10.1177/0261927X20944977.

Kampf, Z. & Danziger, R. (2019). "You dribble faster than Messi and jump higher than Jordan": The art of complimenting and praising in political discourse. *Journal of Politeness Research*, **15**(1), 1–23. https://doi.org/10.1515/pr-2016-0044.

Kampf, Z. & David, Y. (2019). Too good to be true: The effect of conciliatory message design on compromising attitudes in intractable conflicts. *Discourse & Society*, **30**(3), 264–86. https://doi.org/10.1177/0957926519828030.

Kampf, Z., Heimann, G., & Aldar, L. (2022). "These are not just slogans": Assertions of friendship between states. *Journal of Language and Politics*, **21**(5), 653–674. https://doi.org/10.1075/jlp.20079.ald.

Katriel, T. (1986). *Talking Straight: Dugri Speech in Israeli Sabra Culture*. Cambridge: Cambridge University Press.

Katriel, T. (1991). *Communal Webs: Communication and Culture in Contemporary Israel*. Albany: State University of New York Press.

Katriel, T. (1993). Lefargen: A study in Israeli semantics of social relations. *Research on Language and Social Interaction*, **26**(1), 31–53.

Katz, E. & Haas, H. (2001). Twenty years of television in Israel: Are there long-run effects on values and cultural practices? In H. Herzog & E. Ben-Rafael, eds., *Language and Communication in Israel*. Studies of Israeli Society, Vol. 9. New Brunswick, NJ: Transaction Publishers, pp. 313–30.

Kerbrat-Orecchioni, C. (1997). A multilevel approach in the study of talk-in-interaction. *Pragmatics*, **7**(1), 1–20.

Kienpointner, M. (1997). Varieties of rudeness: Types and functions of impolite utterances. *Functions of Language*, **4**(2), 251–87. https://doi.org/10.1075/fol.4.2.05kie.

Kurzon, D. (1998). The speech act status of incitement: Perlocutionary acts revisited. *Journal of Pragmatics*, **29**(5), 571–96. https://doi.org/10.1016/S0378-2166(97)00083-0.

Leech, G. N. (1983). *Principles of Pragmatics*. London: Longman.

Lewandowska-Tomaszczyk, B. (1989). *Praising and Complimenting*. In W. Oleksy, ed., *Contrastic Pragmatics*. Pragmatics and Beyond New Series, Vol. 3. Amsterdam and Philadelphia: John Benjamins, pp. 73–100.

Locher, M. A. (2004). *Power and Politeness in Action: Disagreements in Oral Communication*. Berlin and New York: Mouton de Gruyter.

Locher, M. A. & Graham, S. L. (2010). Introduction to interpersonal pragmatics. In M. A. Locher & S. L. Graham, eds., *Interpersonal Pragmatics*. Berlin: Mouton de Gruyter, pp. 1–13.

Locher, M. A. & Watts, R. J. (2005). Politeness theory and relational work. *Journal of Politeness Research*, **1**(1), 9–33. https://doi.org/10.1515/jplr.2005.1.1.9.

Locher, M. A. & Watts, R. J. (2008). Relational work and impoliteness: Negotiating norms of linguistic behaviour. In D. Bousfield & M. A., Locher, eds., *Impoliteness in Language: Studies on Its Interplay with Power in Theory and Practice*, Vol. 21. Berlin and New York: Mouton de Gruyter, pp. 77–99.

Manes, J. (1983). Compliments: A mirror of culture values. In E. Wolfson & E. Judd, eds., *Sociolinguistics and Language Acquisition*, Rowley, MA: Newbury House, pp. 96–102.

Manes, J. & Wolfson, N. (1981). The compliment formula. In F. Coulmas, ed., *Conversational Routine*, Vol. 2. Berlin and New York: De Gruyter Mouton, pp. 115–32. https://doi.org/10.1515/9783110809145.115.

Maschler, Y. (2001). Veke'ilu haragláyim sh'xa nitka'ot bifním kaze (and like your feet get stuck inside like'): Hebrew kaze (like'), ke'ilu (like'), and the decline of Israeli dugri (direct) speech. *Discourse Studies*, **3**(3), 295–326. https://doi.org/10.1177/1461445601003003003.

McKinnon, C. (1991). Hypocrisy, with a note on integrity. *American Philosophical Quarterly*, **28**(4), 321–30.

Menon, T., Sheldon, O. J., & Galinsky, A. D. (2014). Barriers to transforming hostile relations: Why friendly gestures can backfire. *Negotiation and Conflict Management Research*, **7**(1), 17–37. https://doi.org/10.1111/ncmr.12023.

Mitchell, C. (2000). *Gestures of Conciliation: Factors Contributing to Successful Olive-Branches*. New York: St. Martin's Press.

Mutz, D. C. & Reeves, B. (2005). The new videomalaise: Effects of televised incivility on political trust. *American Political Science Review*, **99**(1), 1–15.

Nelson, G. L., El Bakary, W., & Al Batal, M. (1993). Egyptian and American compliments: A cross-cultural study. *International Journal of intercultural relations*, **17**(3), 293–313.

Ninomiya, H. (2001). Sociability in History In Smelser, N. J., & Baltes, P. B., eds., *International Encyclopedia of the Social and Behavioral Sciences*, Vol. 11. Amsterdam: Elsevier, pp. 14208–14212.

Ogiermann, E. (2015). Direct off-record requests? "Hinting" in family interactions. *Journal of Pragmatics*, **86**, 31–5. https://doi.org/10.1016/j.pragma.2015.06.006.

Ohashi, J. (2008). Linguistic rituals for thanking in Japanese: Balancing obligations. *Journal of Pragmatics*, **40**(12), 2150–74. https://doi.org/10.1016/j.pragma.2008.04.001.

Papacharissi, Z. (2004). Democracy online: Civility, politeness, and the democratic potential of online political discussion groups. *New Media & Society*, **6**(2), 259–83.

Pinto, D. (2011). Are Americans insincere? Interactional style and politeness in everyday America. *Journal of Politeness Research*, **7**(2), 215–38. https://doi.org/10.1515/jplr.2011.011.

Plutarch. ([ca. AD 110–120] 1927). How to tell a flatterer from a friend. In *Moralia*, trans. Frank Cole Babbitt, Vol. 1. Cambridge, MA: Harvard University Press, pp. 261–395.

Rosenblum, A. & Triger, Z. (2007). *Without Words: The Israeli Culture through the Language Mirror*. Or-Yehuda: Dvir [in Hebrew].

Rowbottom, J. (2013). To punish, inform, and criticize: The goals of naming and shaming. In J. Petley, ed., *Media and Public Shaming: Drawing the Boundaries of Disclosure*. London: I. B. Tauris. pp. 1–18.

Ruhi, Ş. & Işık-Güler, H. (2007). Conceptualizing face and relational work in (im)politeness: Revelations from politeness lexemes and idioms in Turkish. *Journal of Pragmatics*, **39**(4), 681–711. https://doi.org/10.1016/j.pragma.2006.11.013.

Schiffrin, D. (1984). Jewish argument as sociability. *Language in Society*, **13**(3), 311–35.

Searle, J. R. (1976). A classification of Illocutionary Acts. *Language in Society*, **5**(1), 1–23. https://doi.org/10.1017/S0047404500006837.

Searle, J. R. & Vanderveken, D. (1985). *Foundations of Illocutionary Logic*. Cambridge: Cambridge University Press.

Sifianou, M. (1992). *Politeness Phenomena in England and Greece: A Cross-Cultural Perspective*. Oxford: Clarendon Press.

Sifianou, M. (2019). Im/politeness and in/civility: A neglected relationship? *Journal of Pragmatics*, **147**, 49–64.

Sorlin, S. (2017). The pragmatics of manipulation: Exploiting im/politeness theories. *Journal of Pragmatics*, **121**, 132–46. https://doi.org/10.1016/j.pragma.2017.10.002.

Sorlin, S. & T. Virtanen (2021). Navigating verbal hypocrisy in face-to-face and mediated contexts: Towards a pragmatic model. Online presentation at the International Pragmatics Research Association Conference, Winterthur, Switzerland, June 27 to July 2.

Spencer-Oatey, H. (2000). *Culturally Speaking: Managing Rapport through Talk Across Cultures*. New York: Continuum.

Spencer-Oatey, H. (2008). Face, (im)politeness and rapport. In H. Spencer-Oatey, ed., *Culturally Speaking: Culture, Communication and Politeness Theory*. London: Continuum, pp. 11–47.

Spencer-Oatey, H. & Kádár, D. Z. (2021). *Intercultural Politeness: Managing Relations across Cultures*. Cambridge: Cambridge University Press.

Stapleton, K. (2020). Swearing and perceptions of the speaker: A discursive approach. *Journal of Pragmatics*, **170**, 381–95.

Steensig, J. (2020). Conversation analysis and affiliation and alignment. In C. Chapelle, ed., *The Concise Encyclopedia of Applied Linguistics*, 1st ed. Wiley-Blackwell. https://learning.oreilly.com/library/view/the-concise-encyclopedia/9781119147367/f03.xhtml#head-2-1.

Steuter, E. & Wills, D. (2010). "The vermin have struck again": Dehumanizing the enemy in post 9/11 media representations. *Media, War & Conflict*, **3**(2), 152–67.

Terkourafi, M. (2015). Conventionalization: A new agenda for im/politeness research. *Journal of Pragmatics*, **86**, 11–18. https://doi.org/10.1016/j.pragma.2015.06.004.

Thomas, J. (1983). Cross-cultural pragmatic failure. *Applied Linguistics*, **4**(2), 91–112.

Thompson, J. B. (2000). *Political Scandal*. Cambridge: Polity.

Tomasello, M. (1999). The human adaptation for culture. *Annual Review of Anthropology*, **28**(1), 509–29.

Vanderveken, D. (1990). *Meaning and Speech Acts, Vol. 1: Principles of Language Use*. Cambridge: Cambridge University Press.

Verschueren, J. (2000). Notes on the role of metapragmatic awareness in language use. *Pragmatics*, **10**(4), 439–56. https://doi.org/10.1075/prag.10.4.02ver.

Vonk, R. (2002). Self-serving interpretations of flattery: Why ingratiation works. *Journal of Personality and Social Psychology*, **82**(4), 515–526.

Watts, R. J. (2003). *Politeness*. Cambridge: Cambridge University Press.

Weizman, E. & Blum-Kulka, S. (1992). Ordinary misunderstanding. In M. Stamenov, ed., *Current Advances in Semantic Theory*. Amsterdam and Philadelphia: John Benjamins, pp. 417–33.

Weizman, E. & Dascal, M. (1991). On clues and cues: Strategies of text-understanding. *Journal of Literary Semantics*, **20**(1), 18–30.

Wierzbicka, A. (1987). *English Speech Act Verbs: A Semantic Dictionary*. Sydney: Academic Press.

Willemsen, L. M., Neijens, P. C., Bronner, F. & de Ridder, J. A. (2011). "Highly Recommended!": The content characteristics and perceived usefulness of online consumer reviews. *Journal of Computer-Mediated Communication*, **17**(1), 19–38. https://doi.org/10.1111/j.1083-6101.2011.01551.x.

Wilson, J. (2002). Political discourse. In D. Schiffrin, D. Tannen, & H. Hamilton, eds., *Handbook of Discourse Analysis*. Oxford: Blackwell, pp. 398–416.

Wodak, R. (2009). *The Discourse of Politics in Action: Politics As Usual*. Basingstoke: Palgrave Macmillan.

Wolfson, N. (1984). Pretty is as pretty does: A speech act view of sex roles. *Applied Linguistics*, **5**(3), 236–44.

Acknowledgments

I wish to thank Zohar Kampf, who is the epitome of *firgun*, for his comments on an earlier version of this Element. I also thank Jonathan Culpeper and Michael Haugh, the editors of this series, and two anonymous reviewers for their valuable comments. Lastly, I want to thank Shahar Berger, for his sincere support.

Cambridge Elements ☰

Pragmatics

Jonathan Culpeper

Lancaster University

Jonathan Culpeper is Professor of English Language and Linguistics in the Department of Linguistics and English Language at Lancaster University, UK. A former co-editor-in-chief of the *Journal of Pragmatics* (2009–14), with research spanning multiple areas within pragmatics, his major publications include: *Impoliteness: Using Language to Cause Offence* (2011, CUP) and *Pragmatics and the English Language* (2014, Palgrave; with Michael Haugh).

Michael Haugh

University of Queensland, Australia

Michael Haugh is Professor of Linguistics and Applied Linguistics in the School of Languages and Cultures at the University of Queensland, Australia. A former co-editor-in-chief of the *Journal of Pragmatics* (2015–2020), with research spanning multiple areas within pragmatics, his major publications include: *Understanding Politeness* (2013, CUP; with Dániel Kádár), *Pragmatics and the English Language* (2014, Palgrave; with Jonathan Culpeper), and *Im/politeness Implicatures* (2015, Mouton de Gruyter).

Advisory Board

About the Series

The Cambridge Elements in Pragmatics series showcases dynamic and highquality original, concise and accessible scholarly works. Written for a broad pragmatics readership it encourages dialogue across different perspectives on language use. It is a forum for cutting-edge work in pragmatics: consolidating theory (especially through cross-fertilization), leading the development of new methods, and advancing innovative topics in pragmatics.

Cambridge Elements $\equiv$

Pragmatics

Elements in the Series

Advice in Conversation
Nele Põldvere, Rachele De Felice and Carita Paradis

Positive Social Acts: The Brighter and Darker Sides of Sociability
Roni Danziger

Pragmatics in Translation: Mediality, Participation and Relational Work
Daria Dayter, Miriam A. Locher and Thomas C. Messerli

Fiction and Pragmatics
Miriam A. Locher, Andreas H. Jucker, Daniela Landert and Thomas C. Messerli

Corpus Pragmatics
Daniela Landert, Daria Dayter, Thomas C. Messerli and Miriam A. Locher

A full series listing is available at: www.cambridge.org/EIPR

Printed in the United States
by Baker & Taylor Publisher Services